The Story Handbook

The Story Handbook

LANGUAGE AND STORYTELLING
FOR LAND CONSERVATIONISTS

Essays by Tim Ahern, William Cronon, John Elder,
Peter Forbes, Barry Lopez, and Scott Russell Sanders

Photo essays by Courtney Bent

Introduction by Will Rogers
Edited by Helen Whybrow

A CENTER FOR LAND AND PEOPLE BOOK

The Trust for Public Land
San Francisco, California

Cover design by Bodenweber Design
Cover photo by Peter Forbes
Book design and production by Helen Whybrow and Jenna Dixon

Printed in the United States of America
Printed with soy-based ink on recycled paper by Queen City Printers

A CENTER FOR LAND AND PEOPLE BOOK
published by
The Trust for Public Land
116 New Montgomery Street
San Francisco, CA 94105
415.495.4014
www.tpl.org

ISBN 0-9672806-2-1
9 8 7 6 5 4 3 2 1

Everything is held together with stories. That is all that is holding us together, stories and compassion.

—Barry Lopez

The value of information does not survive the moment in which it was new. A story is different. It does not expend itself. It preserves and concentrates its strength and is capable of releasing it even after a very long time . . . it resembles the seeds of grain which have lain for centuries in the chambers of the pyramids shut up airtight and have retained their germinative power to this day.

—Walter Benjamin

Contents

Acknowledgments

I was honored and delighted to be asked by Peter Forbes and the Center for Land and People to bring together this handbook on storytelling. Together we would like to thank many people, more than could ever be listed here. A great many people contributed to the evolving ideas behind this book, through their visionary work in the field, through their love of place and the struggle to protect it, through their writing and thinking, and through their witness and belief in the larger vision of land conservation.

Any book that aspires to help with storytelling is deeply indebted to the people and places that inspire the stories. We want to thank the people of Caspar, California; Billerica, Massachusetts; Randolph, New Hampshire; Sterling Forest in New York and New Jersey; Greenwich, Connecticut; Molokai Island, Hawaii; Sante Fe and Chimayo, New Mexico; Central Harlem, New York; and the Nez Perce tribe of Idaho and Oregon. It has been hopeful to see the love of these places expressed so eloquently. We particularly need to thank Gil Griggs, Glenn and Mahealani Davis, Levi Holt, Allen Pinkham, Jaime Pinkham, Carla HighEagle, Louise Griswold, David Willcox, John Scarinza, Walter Graff, Classie Parker, Judy Tarbell, Mike Dell'Ara, and Chris Jinzo.

This book would not have been possible without the staff of the Trust for Public Land who have come to know these places and invested their great energy and talent in helping them to endure. Our special thanks go to Badge Blackett, Tim Northrop, Sonia Jacques, Teresa McHugh, Susan Clark, Alan Front, Jaime Pinkham, Bowen Blair, Marna Schulte, Kate Drahn, Woody Beardsly, Andy Stone, Rose Harvey, Ernest Cook, Laura Baxter,

Scott Parker, Geoff Roach, Erik Kulleseid, Will Rogers, Kelly Huddleston, Deb Frey, David Houghton, Roger Krussman, Donna Smith, and Jenny Parks. Those who contributed to this collection did so with utmost generosity and with wise insight. Thanks to Tim Ahern, Will Rogers, Bill Cronon, John Elder, Peter Forbes, Barry Lopez, and Scott Russell Sanders for their words, and to Courtney Bent for her fine photographs.

Finally, Peter Forbes and I are deeply grateful to all those who helped us shape this book with their vision, craft, and care: Cara Robechek, Kate Williams, Manuel Lebron, Jessie Rogers, Susan Ives, Joanna Bodenweber, Jenna Dixon, Rowan Jacobsen, and Janet Jesso.

Helen Whybrow, Editor

Introduction

| WILL ROGERS

Stories can accomplish what no other form of communication can—they can get through to our hearts with a message. In our world of information transfer, data exchange, and media impressions, where we become callused by so much communication, stories have the power to speak to us about what truly matters. And for land conservationists, what matters more than the relationship between community and the land, between people and place?

True success in our work means moving land conservation out of the "emergency room" of last-ditch efforts, helping our growing communities get control over development by first protecting the places that matter, and reworking our cities so that everyone can feel the touch of nature close to home. To do this we will need to help create a fundamental change in how our society thinks about and treats land; we will need to nurture the flowering of a new land ethic. Stories may be our best way to get there.

I am not talking about the stories we conservationists often tell around the campfire or the water cooler—stories about the challenges of the planning, the funding, or the deal. (And we all know that there are some great stories about the nuts and bolts of how we help save land!) I'm talking of stories about people's relationship with the land and with each other.

Finding these stories is easy. Every place we save has its story. Every place we conserve has its relationships and its connections: the story of a vacant, rubble-strewn lot in Central Harlem that the spirit of one woman and her love for her father turn into an urban oasis of hope and community spirit; the story of homecoming, healing, and restitution as a Native American tribe returns after more than a century to its ancestral homeland, rediscovering its relationship with the land and creating new and positive relationships with the local ranching community; the story of a child's personal discovery and wonder at play in a forest or irrigation ditch that is later threatened with development. In our work we are surrounded by stories about hope, stories about healing, stories about fairness, stories about making a difference, stories about community, stories about connection. And sometimes the best stories of places are about the struggles to save them.

Our challenge lies in using storytelling to stretch our land-saving skills. We are beginning to seek out the stories, find the storytellers, and capture their words and passion so that we can learn to tell their stories ourselves. In this primer on telling the stories of people and place, Peter Forbes and contributors Tim Ahern, William Cronon, John Elder, Barry Lopez, and Scott Russell Sanders help us think about the power of story and how it relates to our work. In the opening essay, Peter makes a powerful argument for the role of stories in helping change how we think about conservation and culture. Barry Lopez writes how authentic stories about land have a way of renewing one's sense of life's purpose. John Elder tells of an experience in the woods near his home that changed the way he thought about his connection to place and the stories of those who lived there before him. Scott Russell Sanders explores our use of certain words— such as *restore, wealth,* and *economy*—whose original "earthy" meanings need to be reclaimed. Bill Cronon argues that our stories of caretaking and an ongoing, changing relationship with the land are ultimately more important than stories of crisis and salvation. And Tim Ahern counsels conservationists on ways to make our message heard more broadly, through the stories we tell to the mainstream media. Interspersed among these essays, "story sheets" describe different TPL projects that have a particularly powerful story to tell. I hope we can learn to harness what is special about land-for-people conservation: that those people whom we are helping to speak powerfully about their love and connection with land will inspire others to do the same.

For those of us who use real-estate tools in the marketplace to conserve land, the term *leverage* has particular meaning— usually with respect to financing deals. Can we use stories to leverage and stretch the on-the-ground impact of our place-saving work? If land conservation, like politics, is fundamentally a local pursuit, can we reach out from a particular place, and use storytelling to carry the impact of our work beyond the property lines? I hope so.

As you read, please view this handbook as a work in progress for us at the Trust for Public Land and hopefully for others in the land trust and conservation community. We welcome your comments, your ideas, and your own experiences. Let's learn together how to build a new land ethic, story by story.

Giving Way to the Story

| PETER FORBES

> The numbers are quickly forgotten. The financial statement must finally give way to the narrative, with all of its exceptions, special cases, imponderables. It must finally give way to the story, which is perhaps the way we arm ourselves against the next and always unpredictable turn of the cycle in the quixotic dare that is life: across the rock and cold of lifelessness, it is our seed, our clove, our filament cast toward the future.
>
> Stanley Crawford, *A Garlic Testament*

It had been snowing in the juniper-piñon woodlands known as Los Manzanares for more than an hour and I was alone, cold and tired. More than once that afternoon I had gotten badly lost in the wooded arroyo, but finally I refound the famous ancient ditch known as the Acequia Madre de San Antonio de Padua and followed it back through the dim light and falling snow to the San Antonio churchyard. I was grateful to see at last the lights of the tiny village of San Antonio. It was just a few days before Christmas, and the twenty or so Hispanic families who lived along Acequia Madre had decorated their homes with luminarias, plastic Santas, and painted crosses. But as I stood in the dirt churchyard that early evening there was only the distant yelp of a dog to keep me company.

I defended myself against the loneliness of the moment by lighting a candle and hunkering down in the backseat of my van to transcribe notes from a week of travel and research. I had seen the famous ditch so beloved it had once caused an armed stand-off between developers and the residents of this New Mexican community, but I had not met those people or directly heard their history. Government officials in Albuquerque had told me, in confiding whispers, that this was the mountain village where Chris Jinzo and his brother Steve had said "enough!", armed themselves with shotguns one early morning in 1998, and stood defiantly between their Acequia Madre de San Antonio and two idling backhoes. Chris and Steve were determined not to let the heavy equipment cross the acequia and enter Los Manzanares to begin construction of thirty upscale homes. The officials who told me this seemed to be anxious about the circumstances of the confrontation but to revel in the outcome: the land encompassing Los Manzanares was never developed. In fact, it was purchased a year later by the Trust for Public Land.

The rap on the window of my van was startling enough to cause me to spill my beer over my notes and topple the candle. The van door swung open and a voice in the dark called out, "This isn't always the safest place for a stranger to camp." But as Chris Jinzo's smiling face emerged from the dark and snow I knew this wasn't true. "You're late for dinner," he said with a laugh, "which isn't the best way to make new friends." I had no idea how Chris knew who I was, but before I could ask him I was sitting in his mother's adobe house being warmed by a fire and listening to their stories:

This valley was settled by the Spanish in 1819, but my family has roots here that go back eight generations to 1789. It doesn't look all that grand or special, but it is. Nearly everyone growing up in this small valley has decided to remain here. Our Acequia Madre de San Antonio isn't a great deal of water, but everyone in this community still drinks from her.

The second Friday and Saturday of June, we clean her. Thirty men head up the arroyo with tools, and the women prepare a big meal in the church. We have the Mattachina Dances the next week with a procession to where the water starts at a spring. This acequia reminds us of our blessings in life. We never take our blessings for granted. Being part of this acequia has, I think, made me see the world differently. It takes some wisdom to know how valuable this place is.

At Thanksgiving, I was walking up the arroyo with most of my family and we saw a cougar on the rocks. She didn't run from us but stood alert and watched and let us pass. I'm so sad for my friends down in Albuquerque who don't know this way of life, who don't have a place that they know and care for. Is it going to get to the point when you'll only see a cougar in the zoo? I'm so scared of that day coming.

The Thanksgiving day that Chris Jinzo saw the cougar in the Sandia Hills of New Mexico, I was much farther west on the island of Molokai, Hawaii, learning about another Trust for Public Land project. At 6:00 A.M. on Thanksgiving morning I was standing in surf facing a rising sun and helping Jaya to pull in his fishnets. I had brought some groceries from town, an hour's drive away on a curvy road, so that Jaya and his family would have some of the basics they needed for Thanksgiving. He said he would gladly trade fish for the bread, cheese, tofu, Hawaiian salt, and avocado that sat in the box in my car. Storm clouds passed over the beach, and a double rainbow hung above the two giant waterfalls cascading over the headwall of the valley.

There were almost no fish in our nets. Jaya was disconcerted at not being able to make the trade and, far more important, at not being able to feed his family that morning. We joked about the three small fish and how we had hoped, maybe, that a turkey would have stumbled into the ocean that morning. After a short walk up the valley to his home in the jungle, Jaya traded me some of their homemade *poi*, a food made from the taro plant that has fed Hawaiians for generations upon generations. Jaya was born twenty-three years ago in Halawa Valley, but until earlier that year he had known almost nothing about this ancient food that once sustained Hawaiian culture.

I had come to Halawa Valley to meet Glenn and Mahealani Davis, two native Hawaiians who were working with the Trust for Public Land to secure the taro fields and reopen them to the old Hawaiian ways of growing food. Glenn is a strong, tall man with the physical grace of a surfer; a skilled fisherman; and a fine craftsman. But on my visit, Glenn walked slowly and unsteadily and often stopped to repeat a story that he had told only minutes before. Three months earlier Glenn had suffered a crippling stroke. Thanksgiving marked his first return to a well-known and beloved place that he carried in his heart and his mind. Glenn's feet knew the trails and led us on long walks through the jungle even though he would sometimes pause in confusion about where he was.

When is land the same as memory? The verb "to remember" suggests becoming a member again, putting something back together, reconnecting to a time or a place. When we conserve land from our past, it gives us the opportunity to remember people and places and our connection to them. We think differently of ourselves when we honor things from before our time. We make sense of ourselves as part of a larger story.

Glenn Davis understands this. A year before his stroke, Glenn sought TPL's help to protect the old taro fields, because he knew that by physically returning to them he would be helping his fellow native Hawaiians remember a lost part of their culture. In the same way, restoring the fields was helping him to restore a part of himself. Even as Glenn's mind failed to give correct order to time and history, the imprint of Halawa Valley was with him forever.

Mahealani Davis showed me an ancient adze and a fishhook

that she found ten years ago in the sand in front of her house. She and Glenn had lived in Halawa Valley for twenty-five years, but it wasn't until they started to find the ancient tools that they understood something about the people who had come before them. Soon thereafter, they realized that the valley was filled with hundreds of overgrown terraces, many of them centuries old. In some ways, Glenn and Mahealani are typical modern Hawaiians. They've relied in the past on tourism for part of their livelihood, and there was a time when they didn't know much about their grandparents' traditions. They felt largely disconnected from the land and their own culture. But the terraced fields, long abandoned, changed their lives forever.

With the Trust for Public Land's help to acquire the terraced land, Glenn and Mahealani Davis have relearned traditions and are rebuilding Hawaiian culture by bringing young Hawaiians back to the taro fields. Until the 1950s taro was a primary food on the islands. The culture developed along with this plant. The word for "family," *ohana,* is also the word for the taro root. *Kuleana* means both "land" and "responsibility." But beginning in the 1950s, many Hawaiians left taro farming and the traditions of their ancestors for jobs in tourism. Returning to the abandoned taro fields reminds young Hawaiians of what their grandparents did, explains their language and customs, and enables them to be more self-sufficient again. And, most important, it brings people together.

Glenn told me, "Hawaiians are beginning to remember that we are organic and part of the land. It's essential for our culture to have places where we can go and remember who we are. Halawa is where you do the understanding. The history is all there imbedded in the land. We just need to uncover it. But you can't protect that land; you can't do anything for that land without the human understanding. We know that this valley was waiting for the people and the understanding to return. Now that we've come back, I mean, now that we've *really* come back and are committed to the taro again, there are more birds singing in the jungle. The water is flowing again. We have come home."

Many stories about the land are quickly recognizable and moving to us because they are stories about relationships. They are about love and loss and healing. Aldo Leopold wrote, "We can be ethical only in relation to something we can see, feel, understand, love, or otherwise have faith in." Scott Russell Sanders responds to Leopold by saying, "This has always struck me as a key justification for art, which brings the world into ethical regard through stories, images, sounds, emotions, and spirit. Leopold is right that we need to *carry the land inside of us,* if we're going to care for it and fight for it. We clearly need science to tell us how the "mechanism" works and how our actions affect the land; but we need art to help us bear the land in mind and heart." Stories, then, are the art to help us bear the land inside of us. They often describe the struggle of finding and keeping one's place in the world.

In 1999 I spent two weeks with the Nez Perce learning about their relationship to land, and in particular about their relationship to the landscape surrounding Chief Joseph Creek in Oregon, lost ancestral land that the Trust for Public Land helped to reconnect them with. Of all the conversation and trips out onto the land, the single event that most helped me to understand the importance of this land to this people was a simple story told to me by Levi Holt, known also as Black Beaver. It is the story of his experience on the day of the dedication and celebration of the Nez Perce's return to the land:

It was a terrible, terrible day. It was raining and overcast and very cold. Many people didn't want to dress in their regalia for fear that the rain would damage it. I decided I would anyway. So I dressed in my ceremonial clothes. This was a very strange day because in many ways it felt very wonderful, but it also felt very sad. It was very heavy on the heart. We couldn't just whip up the horses and stand proud that we had the land. There was something much more there. And I didn't realize that until I actually was on my horse and preparing for the ride to the dedication. As the ceremony down in the valley was getting ready, we were receiving instructions where and when to ride. That's when it came upon me suddenly that I wasn't alone. That my ancestors from the past were riding with me.

Well, my horse—Mengus—and I made a connection, an age-old connection. I believe in our energies, in that spirit between us, and we made this connection that morning, and Mengus rode that trail like a warhorse. Head high, fighting to get to the front. I was the very last rider, so I pushed the crowd because Mengus did not like any of the geldings ahead of me and he was looking to get up there and bite and fight. The rider ahead of me was saying, "Levi, stay to the back."

Well, the beautiful thing about this was, that the third time that Mengus charged up we came into all this mist, and he changed. The horse's composure slowed down, and he was looking and looking like something was with us. And I was wondering if it was the spirit of my people. And as I rode further on my heart became very heavy because of that. And I felt all of the anguish and the pain and the suffering of my people, having to leave that land. The wonderful thing about that land was that it still was with me. It was heavy; this was hard, because that connection gave it back to me. It gave me something. You all [meaning TPL] gave us something. It's hard to explain this spirit feeling that . . . I wasn't alone. I don't remember the ride after that. It was so overwhelming with the rain, the clouds, the drumming way up in the distance. It was like all of those people of the past were riding with me.

So as we believe, things begin here on the land. We went away for a time and now we've come back full circle. Even though it was raining, and the clouds were there, the sun was shining on us. It was a beautiful day and the overwhelming thing was the thunder was coming and the thunder was rolling and it was just loud that day. And it was like Grandfather talking to us. And it was like Grandmother talking to us, in this thunder. As Chief Joseph's name was spoken, this thunder started rolling through the mountain and we felt like all the chiefs were talking. Roar, roar. What a day. What a beautiful, wonderful day.

Hearing Levi Holt's story always makes me pause. An authentic story has power. It makes the listener see the world differently. And stories about our relationship to land have a special power today because they are hopeful antidotes to the unspoken loss that surrounds us. This loss of our bearings gets played out every single day across America. It is the loss of the little places we knew as children, the disappearance of the places that once told us we were home, the dwindling habitat of the grizzly bear and the wolf, the vanishing ways of life, the diminishment of our relationships with the world around us. What we are losing is the world all of us once knew, no matter what our age, the color of our skin, the amount of money in our pocket, or the place where we live. What is dramatically changing is the deep and varied relationships people have had with land, and through land, with a community and a story much bigger than ourselves. A relationship to land is something that every human being experiences positively at a physical or intuitive level. Stories of the land awaken and rekindle these experiences of wholeness inside each and every one of us.

For European Americans, the story of reconnecting with land is plainly different from Native Americans but no less powerful. It is the story of finding a higher expression of oneself, elevating what it means to be human by committing oneself to a place. It is the struggle of stepping out of one's private life to enter into a whole new set of relationships. These are stories of citizenship, because they are about being self-willed; about freedom, fairness, democracy; and, fundamentally, about patriotism.

Craig Barnes now lives in Santa Fe where he has been a strong supporter of the Trust for Public Land's railyard project. The Santa Fe Railyard gathers together Anglo, Hispanic, and Native American values through the creation of a downtown park and public space. Craig told me,

I grew up in the plains of Colorado, and the ability to orient the directions by the mountains and by the stars at night is my resident memory of being close to land, depending on the land, watching the land change from season to season. Those of us who were in any way related to agriculture were always intensely conscious of when the first frost came and when the first green wheat shoots came up in February. Land has an evocative power in the West because of that. And I think also it probably has an evocative power all over the world, because there is something in the human being—like sitting by a fire, watching the waves by the ocean—that is intuitively connected to land. Land does galvanize us more energetically than education or taxes or government corruption. And in a positive way, there's a love for the land. There's an antipathy for taxes, antipathy for corruption, and a fear about schools, but there's a love for the land. And it has the capacity to regenerate us, to re-create us.

This culture throws us back on ourselves. It makes us individual microscopic organisms in a mix of autonomous organisms. It throws us into isolation, makes us lonely. You go to a shopping mall anywhere in Albuquerque or Denver or California, and you feel lonely. You don't feel like you are a part of something larger. We're made lonely by the fact that we are interchangeable marks for value only in terms of what we pay. We don't have as many of the stories that historically human beings would rely on to tell them who they are and that they're bigger than just today's pain. So when we see that little symbol of the old values being sold, it's like selling our chance to be bigger than ourselves.

So what I see the Trust for Public Land doing is more important than buying land and holding it. [This work] is creating a sense of place in time and space that is essential to our mental well-being. I think that stories are part of what we need to tell us who we are. Conservation returns us to our stories. And without our stories we're lonely and cut off again.

The shades of love that people feel for the land, whether they are new to that place or have been there for generations, can be adequately expressed only in terms of human emotion: the expression of our deepest, unspoken values. Telling stories helps conservationists to explain the role that land plays in shaping healthy human lives. Telling stories conveys the emotion, meaning, and power of land conservation's mission. Telling stories is our best hope of reflecting the kind of world we want to live in and, therefore, gives us a hope of creating it.

And, as conservationists, we must tell these stories because they are growing more and more rare and more and more essential to us. Without these stories of connection and relationship, there is increasingly one dominant story to hear and one story to tell. This is the story where the point of trees is board feet, the point of farms is money, the point of people is to be consumers, and the point of other species is largely forgotten. In failing to tell a different story, we fail to express what we really love. In neglecting to express our love, we lose the places that most inspire us. We lose an important part of ourselves.

One of my formative experiences in land conservation happened ten years ago in the rural coastal community of Stonington, Maine. The Trust for Public Land had given the town the opportunity to acquire and protect the fishing pier at Webb's Cove, which had been purchased by a developer and was slated to become six second homes with private docks for yachts. It was from this large stone pier that Stonington may have gotten its name, and from which at least five generations of Stonington families had gone fishing, earned their livelihoods, and shaped their experiences of that place. Clammers and lobstermen launched their boats from this pier; children set traps for minnows beneath it.

Few residents had adequate words to describe why this fishing pier was critical to the community. Many people felt it in their hearts, but this emotion was largely dismissed and unspoken in light of the clear economic arguments about the increased tax revenue that would result from private development. One woman asked a question, though, that I have come to repeat many times. She asked, "When this place is developed and I can no longer go to the pier, I will stand in front of those private, second homes and ask myself, 'What does this place now say about me and my community?'"

I have since learned that the Amish have an even more valuable question that they try to answer before making any change in the land: "What will a change in this land *do* to my family and my neighbors?"

o   o   o

Learning to tell stories starts with learning to hear them. Virtually every conservation project has important stories imbedded within it that we can hear if we slow down enough to listen hard. Here are examples of the elements of stories that we can hear from the people who are connected to a place, and that we need to learn how to retell:

- Stories that reflect our highest aspirations, that show our values
- Stories that show another way of being human
- Stories of hope and possibility
- Stories that show our love and commitment to the diversity of life
- Stories that tell fundamental truths about the world we live in
- Stories of how we would like the world to behave
- Stories that include the wholeness of the human condition, that don't shy away from emotion, conflict, sorrow, joy, love, memory
- Stories about the history of our cultural ideas and practices, our ancestry
- Stories that merge the land and human community
- Stories that are humble, that do not preach
- Stories that give a voice to other people

- ○ Stories of people feeling that they are part of a solution, not part of the problem
- ○ Stories about reclaiming the common wealth, about economics that favor the health of the land

How do we evolve our stories about land conservation to more accurately reflect the kind of world we want to live in? This is a question about shifting the focus from *what* we do and *how* we do it to *why* we do it. It's a question about expanding the audiences to whom we listen and to whom we speak. In trying to listen better and tell different stories, conservation organizations are, in fact, taking an important step in evolving who they are.

Knowing how to distinguish between the facts of *what* we do and the story behind *why* we do it will make conservationists greater leaders. It will help the land conservation movement to create a bigger positive change in culture. Our true mission— that is, showing how land holds enormous transformational value for people—gives rise to a powerful story that goes well beyond the story of *how* we protected the land.

Adding Why to How

How We Conserve Land	Why We Conserve Land
Focus on our tools	Focus on what those tools accomplish
As opportunities arise	Planned to fulfill mission goals
Number of acres saved	Lessons learned, communities changed
Specialized technicians	More broadly focused leaders
Saving parcels of land	Creating a land ethic in people
Recognizing a change in the land	Recognizing a change in people
Creating hope	Giving meaning

One of the great honors and responsibilities of working in land conservation is having the skills and resources to actually accomplish something on the ground. When a community wants to save its last working farm, conservationists must have the skills and abilities to deliver. This emphasis on "how" is powerful; it brings genuine hope to every community in which TPL or any conservation organization works. But when we fail to also focus equally hard on the "why," we leave something very important on the table: we leave behind the larger meaning and cultural significance of our work. By developing real skills in both "how" and "why," land conservationists can deliver both hope and *meaning* to all whom they serve. In adding why to how, land conservationists are becoming leaders by taking more responsibility for what actually happens in the world.

Land conservationists don't want to stop being the highly competent, bold, deal makers who have conserved millions of acres of land. The Trust for Public Land's culture of results, pragmatism, and hope is fundamental to who we are now and who we will be in the future. But we recognize that saving land alone may not be an enduring solution to the current crisis. Many of us are skeptical of the enduring value of saving land without confronting the messy and complex struggle for the soul of our country. We sense that land conservation's great achievements would be leveraged many times over if through our work we could better convey the larger meaning of conservation and its importance in shaping an alternative American culture. We see how the process of saving land, and the meaning of the land itself, can have a greater impact on people's daily lives.

We have already seen that we are transferring more than just land in each of our projects; we are also transferring an element of power, hope, and self-determination to the people who are connected to that land. Now, we need the words and the stories to make this meaning evident to more people.

Every land conservation project is an enactment of a new vision of how to live. Conservationists can be educators by simply making more clear the motive behind protecting a piece of land and then encouraging the stories of that land to be told.

Here's a concrete example of the problem: Forty-five percent of all the local governments in the United States employ some form of land-use control over what owners can and can't do with their land. Of the zoning that exists in the United States, nearly all is based on science or engineering, on factors such as type and slope of soils, size of the building, or the presence of wetlands and critical habitat. Very little zoning uses experience-based criteria, and by that I mean *how people will experience a change in the land.*

Very few laws guide and restrict the development of land based on how it affects people's sense of *belonging.* No laws address how a change to the land affects our hope of community, our network of relationships (human and nonhuman), the memories we build as children, our commitment to a deeper citizenship with where we live, our connection to local culture and traditions. *In short, how will a change in this land affect the wholeness of our community?* None of these questions is part of our land-use laws. We sense what the development of a landscape might do to our families, but we hardly have the words to express it. These questions are just now beginning to guide land conservation, and the answers will come from the best practices of land conservation. We can only begin this critical dialogue by speaking of our connection to the land, by telling stories about the places we love.

Following are points that should be addressed in our stories:

Stories of How	Stories of Why
Tell how the deal was done	Tell about the relationships between the land and people
Speak of the present moment	Speak about the past and the future
Focus on money and law	Express the deeper meaning of the land

Stories of How	Stories of Why
Describe conservation as "holding actions"	Describe how conservation leads to changes in people
Use emergency room language	Use a language of affection/ relationship
Provide short-term solutions	Focus on long- term cultural change

Without doubt, there is an important place for the drama and clarity of stories about how land conservation gets done. Speaking about the threats and risks, the imminent loss of land, the last-minute stopping of the bulldozers, the dramatic negotiations at the last possible hour are all very exciting. Using such "emergency room" rhetoric inspires people to think of conservation-ists as heroes and encourages financial support to conservation organizations.

But along with that exciting emergency room language, we must also develop the ability to speak a language of affection, a language that expresses the powerful land-and-people relation-ships that are the true objective of our endeavor. Jelly Helm and Mark Barden, two premier thinkers in the world of consumer marketing, ask their public-interest clients if the language they use is truly helping to address root problems in society. Stories, they say, are a critical way for people to relate to complex ideas and to "flip a switch that leads them to live their lives differently." Our conservation stories should help people to understand *what really matters and how they can get more of it.*

Environmentalism is often about NO. It tells negative stories with overwhelming and abstract facts that depress people, offer few solutions, and leave us feeling powerless. Land conserva-tion stories can be daringly positive, simple but with a grand vision, and rewarding, and they can connect people directly to solutions. Imagine if every story that conservationists told about the land helped people to see what really matters and how they can get more of it.

o   o   o

One very hot Saturday in July, I found myself on 121st Street in Central Harlem trying to get perspective. For an hour or more I sat on the corner of Frederick Douglass Avenue eating peaches and taking in the neighborhood. There was constant motion everywhere: motorcycles racing each other down the avenue, vendors selling sunglasses and old record albums, children playing games at my feet, an endless flow of people. But amid all the noise and pavement and broken glass, there was a quiet green garden. An eight-foot-high chain-link fence could barely keep the sunflowers from pouring out into 121st Street. With two large townhouses protecting either flank, the garden itself was just plain bold and beautiful. A dozen discarded lawn chairs had been retrieved and organized loosely around leaning tables and empty crates as if a card game or a good meal had just been finished. I could see rows of corn, plots of vegetables, climbing snap peas, grapevines, fruit trees, and a dogwood. I could hear birds. Men and women of all ages were hanging on the chain-link fence talking to friends on the street, and then quickly turning back into the garden with a hoe or a laugh.

Five Star is breathtakingly beautiful and heavy with life. It is stewardship and wildness wrapped together and dropped down on 121st Street. Classie Parker, a third-generation resident of this neighborhood, produces food, beauty, tolerance, neighborliness, and a relationship to land for people throughout her part of Harlem, all on less than one-quarter of an acre. Five Star Garden is almost absurdly small, but for the people of 121st Street —who, for the most part, never leave Harlem—the garden is their own piece of land to which they have developed a very deep personal attachment. These are Classie's words:

> Once I started working with the earth, the love in people started coming out. People I didn't even know, strangers literally would come in and say, "Oh, I love this." And they started

telling me their life stories . . . where they came from, how old they were when they first started. They were telling me things that they didn't even tell their own people. So it was like a healing for them, too. When they left they seemed changed. One was the lady with Alzheimer's. She and her aide were walking by one day, and they saw the garden so they decided to come in. We didn't know she had Alzheimer's but the aide knew. And within thirty days the lady made a complete change. When she first came the lady seemed listless, like living in her own world. And the other seniors started talking to her, acting like it was a natural thing. And pretty soon she started talking back to them. This lady, come to find out, was a dancer with the burlesque dancers back in the 1930s and she got up and she showed us how she used to kick her leg and tell us about all the pretty things she was wearing. One night, this lady's son came and only Daddy was here at the garden. And he said, "I just come to see if this thing . . . if this garden is real. Because I cannot believe the change that has occurred in my mother."

We think of ourselves as farmers, city farmers. Never environmentalists. We love plants, we love being with the earth, working with the earth. But there is something here in this garden for everyone. And any race, creed, or color . . . now, can you explain that? This is one of the few places in Harlem where they can be free to be themselves. It's hard to put into words what moves people to come in this garden and tell us their life stories, but it happens every day. There's love here. People gonna go where they feel the flow of love.

There is a difference. You come in here and sit down, Peter, don't you feel comfortable with us? Don't you feel you're free to be you? That we're not going to judge you because you're a different color or because you're a male? Do you feel happy here? Do you feel intimidated? Don't you feel like my dad's your dad?

Classie boiled it all down: "Don't you feel like my dad is your dad?" I remember laughing as Classie said this, and I paused from our work to look up at her father, sitting ten feet across from me with his feet firmly planted on the earth, both hands resting on canes, eighty-seven years old, garden dirt on his face. What we had in common at that moment was profound: it was that soil and that place and the love and hope that Classie could wish for both of us.

The Trust for Public Land's mission has always been about connecting land and people. As we come to understand this great mission more and more, we cannot help but recognize the critical place of relationships in our conservation mission. And by relationships I mean dependencies and reliances among people, among species, between the whole of the land community. So perhaps what we are looking for is *a language of relationships.*

Aldo Leopold said, "There are two things that interest me: the relationship of people to each other, and the relationship of people to the land." Fifty years after Leopold's death, conservationists are still struggling to rethink the promise of land conservation as a force for social reform that heals people and culture by creating relationships between people and the land that positively transforms both.

Viewing land as the place of relationships requires that conservationists firmly put their work in a context of time and history. What we are "saving" is not so much the piece of land but the quality and integrity of our relationship to the land so that what we will and *will not do* is preserved in perpetuity. If we're lucky, the land will evolve and change forever, but it's our human attitude—our values—that most need to be "protected." Our laws protect land *from* us when we are at our worst rather than keep us together when we are at our best. The only way for a culture to stop viewing land as a commodity is to stop thinking of land as an object and to begin thinking of it subjectively, as us. In a conservation movement guided by relationships, our most valued natural areas would be described as an expression of ourselves *at our best.*

Those conservationists working at connecting land and people have some very powerful relationships to talk about that most people, no matter their background or their race, will recognize and respond to positively. Following are some of the themes of integration found in land conservation that can inspire people to live differently.

Thinking about the whole. When conservation takes responsibility for the whole, from inner city to wilderness, it speaks biological truths, serves to connect landscapes, and educates people about critical interdependencies. A whole natural system, including humans, is what conservation ought to protect.

Protecting what people love. Conservation should highlight people's shared values and their local passion for what they know and love. This brings people together and helps them fear one another less. By protecting what people love, we offer a positive vision of the world we want to live in.

Integration of healthy land and healthy people. Conservation is about economic, mental, physical, and spiritual well being. It's often about healing ourselves and other life. Through this view of life as one healthy whole, restoration of land and of oneself become the same.

Striving for fairness. Conservation's impact becomes more profound as it serves all people, regardless of income, color, or where one lives. Everyone needs and deserves a relationship with the land. Similarly, it is fair and moral for conservation to honor the gift of all life, not just human life, and to respect the life, health and independence of many ecosystems.

Honoring home. By focusing on where people live, work and play, conservation protects the places that enable us to think about who we are and where we belong. It roots us, and helps us to better value and appreciate the places immediately around us. The work of local conservation provides the daily reminders that what we do to the land we do to ourselves.

Conservationists must appeal to human consciousness in every project we undertake. We must appeal to people on economic terms, aesthetic terms, but also on moral and emotional grounds. We must reach people's hearts and minds, and the most powerful way we might do this is by offering an integrated story of people and the land. We believe that our conservation mission does speak directly to many people's values, and that by bearing our mission into the world we expand those values into the culture. Through stories, we can translate the soul of the land into the soul of our culture.

Story Sheets | An Introduction

Story sheets are simple, straightforward ways of explaining the meaning of a conservation project or program. One should be able to capture and convey the story and the meaning with one photograph and two pages or less of text.

You will quickly discover from the examples that follow that there is no one story for a project. A diversity of stories, in fact, means a rich and complex conservation project. Story sheets shouldn't follow a formula, but should be responsive to the story itself. There are, however, some helpful guidelines, which are listed below. You might also find the annotations of these story sheet examples to be helpful.

1. Describe the place from personal experience and through the words of someone who lives there.

2. Briefly state the context—or the core ideas—for the conservation project or program.

3. Offer the broader historical context for the project.

4. In telling the conservation part of the story, state the larger social good that is achieved through this project, and the guiding themes that make it distinct from other projects.

5. Pay attention to language, and point out words that best convey the relationships strengthened and preserved by this project.

6. Let someone else's words find the metaphor and emotion that convey the greatest power and core values of the conservation effort.

7. Less is more.

Interspersed throughout this book are annotated story sheets for three TPL projects: New York's Urban Gardens, the Halawa Valley of Hawaii, and the Nez Perce Precious Lands in Oregon. Unannotated story sheets describe three other projects: Caspar Headlands in northern California, Pond of Safety in Randolph, New Hampshire, and Sterling Forest on the New York–New Jersey border.

Five Star Garden | A Story of Overcoming Difference

The corner of 121st Street and Frederick Douglass Avenue is a very busy place.[1] Motorcycles race each other down the avenue, vendors sell sunglasses and old record albums, children play games on the sidewalk amid an endless flow of people. Surrounded by all the noise and pavement is[2] a quiet green garden that can barely keep the sunflowers from pouring out into 121st Street. Step inside and you'll see rows of corn, plots of vegetables, climbing snap peas, grapevines, fruit trees, and hear birds. Men and women of all ages are hanging on the chain-link fence talking to friends on the street.

Classie Parker started Five Star Garden[3] in Central Harlem because she felt stuck on a street where no one knew anyone else and where drug dealers ran everything. She especially feared for her father, who was growing old and needed a way to stay active and get outside. Classie's apartment stood adjacent to a 3,600-square-foot vacant lot that was crowded with garbage of every kind. Classie got the idea to create a garden on that lot as a place where the old and young could work together. Classie says, "Once I started working with the earth, the love in people started coming out. People I didn't even know, strangers

PHOTO: PETER FORBES

literally would come in and say, 'Oh, I love this.' And they started telling me their life stories . . . they were telling me things they didn't even tell their own people."

This work is about much more than open space protection.[4] It is about the power of land to nurture stronger communities. In 1999, 113 community gardens in New York City were put up for sale to be built upon. Working with dozens of community groups and activists, TPL arranged to acquire sixty-two of these lots from the city so that they could remain community gardens. TPL is now creating three borough land trusts, including a Manhattan Land Trust, to be the long-term stewards for the property.

For as long as there have been cities, there have been people in those cities who have sought out land and soil to grow their own food, to play, and to connect with nature.[5] TPL has been working since 1978 to make land available to people in the five boroughs of New York.[6] In this program, TPL is making land available for gardens and kids' playgrounds on vacant lots once unavailable to the community.

Five Star is beautiful and heavy with life. It is stewardship and wildness[7] wrapped together and dropped down on a busy city street. Classie and her neighbors produce food, beauty, tolerance, neighborliness, and a relationship to land for people throughout her part of Harlem, all on less than one-quarter of an acre.[8] These are Classie's words:[9]

> We think of ourselves as farmers, city farmers. Never environmentalists. We love plants, we love being with the earth, working with the earth. But there is something here in this garden for everyone. And any race, creed, or color . . . now, can you explain that? This is one of the few places in Harlem where they can be free to be themselves. There's love here. People gonna go where they feel the flow of love. There is a difference. You come in here and sit down; don't you feel comfortable with us? That we're not going to judge you because you're a different color or because you're a male? Do you feel happy here? Do you feel intimidated? Don't you feel like my dad's your dad?[10]

Notes

1. Describe the place as carefully as you can and from personal experience. If you haven't been there and seen the place you are talking about, your readers will have a hard time envisioning it. Enable the reader/listener to understand the place by feeling its character.
2. When telling the story, use the present tense.
3. Tell the story of the entire program or project through one example. This is an attempt to make the project/program more real by boiling it down to individual human stories. It removes the abstractions and jargon of "conservation talk." Don't worry that the person or story you choose is not perfectly representative of your program. Tell two stories if you need to reflect another idea.
4. State what makes this project different from or similar to other projects/programs. What are the guiding themes of this work? Try to summarize the "big picture" purpose of the work.
5. Put the conservation work in a broader historical context.
6. Give the history of the TPL project or program in succinct language.
7. Restate the context of the story again. Why is this story important? What is this story really about?
8. Bring the contextual themes to light without using any conservation jargon. This is a story about fairness, equity, and how land conservation impacts human lives, but the storyteller tries to convey that through Classie Parker's perspective, not professional language.
9. Tell the story through a person's exact words without filters of any kind. Its power as a story comes from the authenticity and spontaneity of their words.
10. This single line "Don't you feel like my dad's your dad?" is the whole story of the urban gardening program. It explains in deeply simple and intuitive terms the role that land can play in urban gardens to bring different people together. The interviewer for this story (Peter Forbes) spent a single day with Classie getting to know her life story, the garden, and how the two were interconnected. Those conversations were taped and transcribed and resulted in forty pages of dialogue. There were many stories that could be used to explain the importance of the gardens, but this is the one that most surprised and moved the interviewer. Don't be afraid to choose the story that most moves you. If you are not surprised and moved by the encounter, your story will not be surprising and moving to others. The most valuable thing any story can convey is our deepest emotions.

Landscape and Narrative

| BARRY LOPEZ

One summer evening in a remote village in the Brooks Range of Alaska, I sat among a group of men listening to hunting stories about the trapping and pursuit of animals. I was particularly interested in several incidents involving wolverine, in part because a friend of mine was studying wolverine in Canada, among the Cree, but, too, because I find this animal such an intense creature. To hear about its life is to learn more about fierceness.

Wolverines are not intentionally secretive, hiding their lives from view, but they are seldom observed. The range of their known behavior is less than that of, say, bears or wolves. Still, that evening no gratuitous details were set out. This was somewhat odd, for wolverine easily excite the imagination; they can loom suddenly in the landscape with authority, with an aura larger than their compact physical dimensions, drawing one's immediate and complete attention. Wolverine also have a deserved reputation for resoluteness in the worst winters, for ferocious strength. But neither did these attributes induce the men to embellish.

I listened carefully to these stories, taking pleasure in the sharply observed detail surrounding the dramatic thread of events. The story I remember most vividly was about a man hunting a wolverine from a snow machine in the spring. He followed the animal's tracks for several miles over rolling tundra in a certain valley. Soon he caught sight ahead of a dark spot on the crest of a hill—the wolverine pausing to look back. The hunter was catching up, but each time he came over a rise the wolverine was looking back from the next rise, just out of range. The hunter topped one more rise and met the wolverine bounding toward him. Before he could pull his rifle from its scabbard the wolverine flew across the engine cowl and the windshield, hitting him square in the chest. The hunter scrambled his arms wildly, trying to get the wolverine out of his lap, and fell over as he did so. The wolverine jumped clear as the snow machine rolled over, and fixed the man with a stare. He had not bitten, not even scratched the man. Then the wolverine walked away. The man thought of reaching for the gun, but no, he did not.

The other stories were like this, not so much making a point as evoking something about contact with wild animals that would never be completely understood.

When the stories were over, four or five of us walked out of the home of our host. The surrounding land, in the persistent light of a far northern summer, was still visible for miles—the striated, pitched massifs of the Brooks Range; the shy, willow-lined banks of the John River flowing south from Anaktuvuk Pass; and the flat tundra plain, opening with great affirmation to the north. The landscape seemed alive because of the stories. It was precisely these ocherous tones, this kind of willow, exactly this austerity that had informed the wolverine narratives. I felt exhilaration, and a deeper confirmation of the stories. The mundane tasks which awaited me I anticipated now with pleasure. The stories had renewed in me a sense of the purpose of my life.

o   o   o

This feeling, an inexplicable renewal of enthusiasm after story-telling, is familiar to many people. It does not seem to matter greatly what the subject is, as long as the context is intimate and the story is told for its own sake, not forced to serve merely as the vehicle for an idea. The tone of the story need not be solemn. The darker aspects of life need not be ignored. But I think intimacy is indispensable—a feeling that derives from the listener's trust and a storyteller's certain knowledge of this subject and regard for his audience. This intimacy deepens if the storyteller tempers his authority with humility, or when terms of idiomatic expression, or at least the physical setting for the story, are shared.

I think of two landscapes—one outside the self, the other within. The external landscape is the one we see—not only the line and color of the land and its shading at different times of the day, but also its plants and animals in season, its weather, its geology, the record of its climate and evolution. If you walk up, say, a dry arroyo in the Sonoran Desert you will feel a mounding and rolling of sand and silt beneath your foot that is distinctive. You will anticipate the crumbling of the sedimentary earth in the arroyo bank as your hand reaches out, and in that tangible evidence you will sense a history of water in the region. Perhaps a black-throated sparrow lands in a paloverde bush—the resiliency of the twig under the bird, that precise shade of yellowish-green against the milk-blue sky, the fluttering whir of the arriving sparrow, are what I mean by "the landscape." Draw on the smell of creosote bush, or clack stones together in the dry air. Feel how light is the desiccated dropping of the kangaroo rat. Study an animal track obscured by the wind. These are all elements of the land, and what makes the landscape comprehensible are the relationships between them. One learns a landscape finally not by knowing the name or identity of everything in it, but by perceiving the relationships in it—like that between the sparrow and the twig. The difference between the relationships and the elements is the same as that between written history and a catalog of events.

The second landscape I think of is an interior one, a kind of projection within a person of a part of the exterior landscape. Relationships in the exterior landscape include those that are named and discernible, such as the nitrogen cycle, or a vertical sequence of Ordovician limestone, and others that are uncodified or ineffable, such as winter light falling on a particular kind of granite, or the effect of humidity on the frequency of a blackpoll warbler's burst of song. That these relationships have purpose and order, however inscrutable they may seem to us, is a tenet of evolution. Similarly, the speculations, intuitions, and formal ideas we refer to as "mind" are a set of relationships in the interior landscape with purpose and order; some of these are obvious, many impenetrably subtle. The shape and character of these relationships in a person's thinking, I believe, are deeply influenced by where on this earth one goes, what one touches, the patterns one observes in nature—the intricate history of one's life in the land, even a life in the city, where wind, the chirp of birds, the line of a falling leaf, are known. These thoughts are arranged, further, according to the thread of one's moral, intellectual, and spiritual development. The interior landscape responds to the character and subtlety of an exterior landscape; the shape of the individual mind is affected by land as it is by genes.

In stories like those I heard at Anaktuvuk Pass about wolverine, the relationship between separate elements in the land is set forth clearly. It is put in a simple framework of sequential incidents and apposite detail. If the exterior landscape is limned well, the listener often feels that he has heard something pleasing and authentic—trustworthy. We derive this sense of confidence I think not so much from verifiable truth as from an understanding that lying has played no role in the narrative. The storyteller is obligated to engage the reader with a precise vocabulary, to set forth a coherent and dramatic rendering of incidents—and to be ingenuous. When one hears a story one takes pleasure in it for different reasons—for the euphony of its phrases, an aspect of the plot, or because one identifies with one of the characters. With certain stories certain individuals may experience a deeper, more profound sense of well-being. This latter phenomenon, in my understanding, rests at the heart of storytelling as an elevated experience among aboriginal peoples. It results from bringing two landscapes together. The exterior landscape is organized according to principles or laws or tendencies beyond human control. It is understood to contain an integrity that is beyond human analysis and unimpeachable. Insofar as the storyteller depicts various subtle and obvious relationships in the exterior landscape accurately in his story, and insofar as he orders them along traditional lines of meaning to create the narrative, the narrative will "ring true." The listener who "takes the story to heart" will feel a pervasive sense of congruence within himself and also with the world.

Among the Navajo and, as far as I know, many other native peoples, the land is thought to exhibit a sacred order. That order is the basis of ritual. The rituals themselves reveal the power in that order. Art, architecture, vocabulary, and costume, as well as ritual, are derived from the perceived natural order of the universe—from observations and meditations on the exterior landscape. An indigenous philosophy—metaphysics, ethics, epistemology, aesthetics, and logic—may also be derived from a people's continuous attentiveness to both the obvious (scientific) and ineffable (artistic) orders of the local landscape. Each individual, further, undertakes to order his interior landscape according to the exterior landscape. To succeed in this means to achieve a balanced state of mental health.

I think of the Navajo for a specific reason. Among the various sung ceremonies of this people—Enemyway, Coyoteway, Red Antway, Uglyway—is one called Beautyway. In the Navajo view, the elements of one's interior life—one's psychological makeup and moral bearing—are subject to a persistent principle of disarray. Beautyway is, in part, a spiritual invocation of the order of the exterior universe, that irreducible, holy complexity that manifests itself as all things changing through time (a Navajo definition of beauty, hózhǫ́ǫ́). The purpose of this invocation is to re-create in the individual who is the subject of the Beauty-way ceremony that same order, to make the individual again a reflection of the myriad enduring relationships of the landscape.

I believe story functions in a similar way. A story draws on relationships in the exterior landscape and projects them onto the interior landscape. The purpose of storytelling is to achieve harmony between the two landscapes, to use all the elements of story—syntax, mood, figures of speech—in a harmonious way to reproduce the harmony of the land in the individual's interior. Inherent in story is the power to reorder a state of psychological confusion through contact with the pervasive truth of those relationships we call "the land."

o   o   o

These thoughts, of course, are susceptible to interpretation. I am convinced, however, that these observations can be applied to the kind of prose we call nonfiction as well as to traditional narrative forms such as the novel and the short story, and to some poems. Distinctions between fiction and nonfiction are sometimes obscured by arguments over what constitutes "the truth." In the aboriginal literature I am familiar with, the first ·distinction made among narratives is to separate the authentic from the inauthentic. Myth, which we tend to regard as fictitious or "merely metaphorical," is as authentic, as real, as the story of a wolverine in a man's lap. (A distinction is made, of course, about the elevated nature of myth—and frequently the circumstances of myth-telling are more rigorously prescribed than those for the telling of legends or vernacular stories—but all of these narratives are rooted in the local landscape. To violate *that* connection is to call the narrative itself into question.)

The power of narrative to nurture and heal, to repair a spirit in disarray, rests on two things: the skillful invocation of unimpeachable sources and a listener's knowledge that no hypocrisy or subterfuge is involved. This last simple fact is to me one of the most imposing aspects of the Holocene history of man. We are more accustomed now to thinking of "the truth" as something that can be explicitly stated, rather than as something that can be evoked in a metaphorical way outside science and Occidental culture. Neither can truth be reduced to aphorism or formulas. It is something alive and unpronounceable. Story creates an atmosphere in which it becomes discernible as a pattern. For a storyteller to insist on relationships that do not exist is to lie. Lying is the opposite of story. (I do not mean to confuse ignorance with deception, or to imply that a storyteller can perceive all that is inherent in the land. Every storyteller falls short of a perfect limning of the landscape—perception and language both fail. But to make up something that is not there, something which can never be corroborated in the land, to knowingly set forth a false relationship, is to be lying, no longer telling a story.)

Because of the intricate, complex nature of the land, it is not always possible for a storyteller to grasp what is contained in a story. The intent of the storyteller, then, must be to evoke, honestly, some single aspect of all that the land contains. The storyteller knows that because different individuals grasp the story at different levels, the focus of his regard for truth must be at the primary one—with who was there, what happened, when, where, and why things occurred. The story will then possess similar truth at other levels—the integrity inherent at the primary level of meaning will be conveyed everywhere else. As long as the storyteller carefully describes the order before him, and uses his storytelling skill to heighten and emphasize certain relationships, it is even possible for the story to be more successful than the storyteller himself is able to imagine.

o   o   o

I would like to make a final point about the wolverine stories I heard at Anaktuvuk Pass. I wrote down the details afterward, concentrating especially on aspects of the biology and ecology of the animals. I sent the information on to my friend living with the Cree. When, many months later, I saw him, I asked whether the Cree had enjoyed these insights of the Nunamiut into the nature of the wolverine. What had they said?

"You know," he told me, "how they are. They said, 'That could happen.'"

In these uncomplicated words the Cree declared their own knowledge of the wolverine. They acknowledged that although they themselves had never seen the things the Nunamiut spoke of, they accepted them as accurate observations, because they did not consider story a context for misrepresentation. They also preserved their own dignity by not overstating their confidence in the Nunamiut, a distant and unknown people. Whenever I think of this courtesy on the part of the Cree I think of the dignity that is ours when we cease to demand the truth and realize that the best we can have of those substantial truths that guide our lives is metaphorical—a story. And the most of it we are likely to discern comes only when we accord one another the respect the Cree showed the Nunamiut. Beyond this—that the interior landscape is a metaphorical representation of the exterior landscape, that the truth reveals itself most fully not in dogma but in the paradox, irony, and contradictions that distinguish compelling narratives—beyond this there are only failures of imagination: reductionism in science; fundamentalism in religion; fascism in politics.

Our national literatures should be important to us insofar as they sustain us with illumination and heal us. They can always do that so long as they are written with respect for both the source and the reader, and with an understanding of why the human heart and the land have been brought together so regularly in human history.

Precious Lands | A Story of Healing

The story of how TPL helped to reunite the Nez Perce tribe with their homeground in Wallowa County, Oregon, is a story of cultural and personal healing. For a people, it returns the Nez Perce to their ancestral grounds from which they were removed more than 125 years ago during the time of the Indian wars.

Allen Pinkham, former chairman of the Nez Perce tribal council, explained, "Every time we spoke up for our rights, not only our human rights but our civil rights, something was taken away from us. So to be more self-sufficient, to be more ourselves, we have chosen to rebuild our lives around the earth. This, alone, will make us stronger and give us back our self-respect that no one can then take away. Yes, we need schools and jobs. But the best way for the Nez Perce to fight drug abuse and alcoholism is to restore the salmon, and to bring back the wolves, and to ride across the land on our own Appaloosa."

TPL works with tribes all over the United States to preserve and promote the unique land-based culture of American Indians. By protecting sites of traditional value, ensuring tribal access to the land, and often placing property directly under tribal stewardship, TPL helps Native

communities restore their spiritual, cultural, and economic relationship to the land.

For individual Nez Perce, returning to the Precious Lands offers more of a foothold in the web of life to which he or she seeks to return. The return of the Nez Perce to the lands around Joseph Creek enables future generations to inherit not just the memory of their ancestors but also a sense of their unique and cherished way of life and the choice to practice some of that way of life.

Carla HighEagle put it this way:

> The land holds the spiritual aspect of everything that is living. Everything that's on it. Everything that's crossed it has left a part of himself there. Everything that's died and been reborn is there in the land. And as people we became disconnected from that. We bought into another story. We don't recognize it anymore. We don't value it. Some people see a tree and say, "Well, that's worth so many million board feet," or whatever. They don't see it as a connected part of themselves. That's the tie that's been broken, and buying the Precious Lands reestablishes that tie. Not in terms of management plans and goals and objectives for the year, but in terms of who we are. It's important to correct the things you can in your life, and land offers the most healing because it connects us to nature and to one another.[1]

Note

1. Many of the most successful conservation projects and programs hold the seeds of multiple stories. The Precious Lands project is such a case. In fact, every project can have multiple stories based on who tells them and what their experience of the land is all about.

   The interviewer (Peter Forbes) collected this story and the one that follows during a two-week stay with the Nez Perce. Some distinct themes, such as healing and neighborliness, emerged in the interviews, and these stories are told by grouping quotes and details together to reflect those themes. As an experiment in the power of stories, read these Precious Lands stories together and determine for yourself which is the more meaningful to you. Why is it more meaningful?

Precious Lands | A Story of Neighborliness

For a people that were forcefully removed from their land five generations ago, to be a good neighbor requires a supreme act of forgiveness.
The return of the Nez Perce to their Precious Lands in 1997 has helped
to inspire that forgiveness in everyone. The story of how TPL helped to
reconnect the Nez Perce with the 10,000-acre Precious Lands is a story
of cultural and personal healing. It is also direct evidence of the power of
land conservation to create social change within a community.

Allen Pinkham, former chairman of the Nez Perce tribal council,
spoke for his tribe when he said, "Returning to this land allows us to
practice being good neighbors again. Our neighbors are the salmon and
the eagle and the wolves and, yes, particularly the white ranchers and
even their ancestors who killed our ancestors and drove us off our land.
The land teaches how we must all live together as good neighbors."

In 1997, the largely white community of Enterprise, Oregon, started
thinking and acting differently because of the return of the Nez Perce.
Many debated the appropriateness of the high school's mascot, the Sav-
ages, when the Nez Perce became the new neighbors in town, and they
eventually decided to do away with the Indian caricature that adorned

their building and basketball floor. The school board initiated a six-month community discussion about race, civility, and community life. The Nez Perce partnered with white ranchers and irrigators to restore salmon to the local rivers, an initiative that shares control of the river and makes neighbors out of salmon.

Carla HighEagle says,

> There is a promise you make when you're born to the Creator that says, "I will tell the truth. I will honor my family. I have a responsibility to the earth and to all those around me in everything that I do." The salmon is the same way. He was given instructions when he was born in the headwaters, and as he grew, that he would migrate down and he would be in the ocean and he would come back over the falls to achieve that purpose of coming back—to spawn and start the cycle of life over again—and his body would provide nourishment for everything that was there in the environment. That's the cycle of who you are. The land also recognizes and celebrates that same cycle. Every day. Coming home to the Precious Lands has enabled us to forgive and forget, to do what we must do as good neighbors.

Storytelling for the Media

THE SANTUORIO DE CHIMAYO STORY

| TIM AHERN

During Easter weekend, 2002, millions of people around the nation read the moving story of the successful effort to save the open space and lands around the Santuorio de Chimayo, a small Catholic mission church in northern New Mexico.

For two hundred years, the small wooden church has drawn visitors—many of them pilgrims known as "penitentes" who walk from as far away as Albuquerque, ninety miles to the south. The legend of the Chimayo mission began when it was built where a crucifix was supposedly found; over the years, numerous visitors have claimed miraculous cures, attributed to the earth from the mission floor.

Because of those cures, the mission is known as the "Lourdes of America," and hundreds of thousands of people visit it annually. The bulk of these visitors come during Holy Week, the seven days preceding Easter and the holiest time of the year for Christians.

The Santuorio is the central building of Chimayo, a small village in the Sangre de Cristo Mountains northeast of Santa Fe. Chimayo is facing the same development pressures that are changing the landscape all across New Mexico and the West. Land that has been owned by families and passed down from generation to generation is being broken up and sold. At Chimayo, the parcels behind the church, originally held by a single family, have been split up among family members.

Jenny Parks, a project manager in the Trust for Public Land's Southwestern office, has been working with landowners to buy the open land behind the Santuorio. Encroaching development threatens to spoil the pastoral views that worshipers now look out on when they sit on the stone benches where outdoor mass is held during warm weather.

In late January, Jenny sat down with me and Jay Dean, TPL's vice president for marketing. She told us the story of her project and the story of Chimayo. As Jenny talked about how the pilgrimages to Chimayo reach a crescendo during Holy Week, it became obvious to me that Easter was the best time to interest the media in our story. As a former journalist, I knew the Easter weekend was often a "slow" time for news, and that during that time the media would be seeking Easter-related stories.

In thinking about the Chimayo story, we quickly realized that it been told many times, in many ways, by the media. What we needed was a new "hook"—something to respond with when the media said, "Yes, yes, I've seen the Chimayo story, what do you have that is new and different?" What we had that was "new" was our effort—a successful one—to preserve the open fields behind the church and so, too, preserve the little mission's pastoral character.

Jenny, along with Kate Drahn and Jeanette Alt in the Southwest region's public affairs office, provided all the details of the land transactions. Then, beyond those numbers and statistics, we set out to gather the human stories that would provide the media with the compelling drama of the effort to save the land around the famous little Spanish church in the valley.

The four of us compiled lists of people who lived near the mission or who had worked on the preservation effort. We interviewed them all, taking extensive notes as they talked about the mission and the meaning it had for them.

For example, Leona Medine-Tiede now runs a large business in Sante Fe, selling tortillas. But she began decades ago, selling homemade tortillas from a small stand across the dirt road from the mission. Now, she returns to Chimayo each year during Holy Week to feed the penitentes as they end their pilgrimage.

"Over the years, this place hasn't changed much," she told me. "When I was growing up here, I could look down across the fields behind the mission and see cattle and horses, and it seemed timeless. That is how it should be preserved for all the people who come here. To see homes or trailers built on the land behind the mission, that wouldn't be right. That would be awful."

Ray Bal, one of Leona's neighbors, owns a small gift shop near the front of the church. He also owns one of the parcels of land behind the mission. "A long time ago, this land was used as a gathering spot for the Native Americans who lived here. This land is sacred because of all the people who have lived here, and it should never be desecrated. Saving this land is about more than keeping space open. It is about preserving a way of life, a way we have lived on this land here for generations."

With our interviews from Bal, Medine-Tiede, and others, we prepared a package of background material for the media, including factual data about the transactions, previous media stories about the mission, and a list of people who could be interviewed—along with a preview of what they would say. In preparing this material, we were guided by what we knew the media would be looking for.

We then began contacting media, inviting coverage of the story. In our pitch, we focused on the Easter connection. And we worked with the media throughout their reporting process, answering questions and digging up additional facts as the stories developed. For example, we were aware that the Associated Press (AP)—the world's largest and oldest news-gathering organization—has many and varied levels of coverage. We knew that the story would be picked up by reporters from the Santa Fe office, which is the bureau nearest to Chimayo. The AP office there routinely covers the Chimayo pilgrimage every Easter and distributes the story throughout New Mexico. Some years, the story is sent to a wider distribution list, throughout the Rocky Mountain region. We wanted the AP to "nationalize" the story —that is, to have the Santa Fe bureau write a story that would be sent throughout the country, to the AP's entire network of thousands of outlets. As part of that effort—which turned out to be successful—we told the "larger" story of Chimayo, emphasizing how TPL protects similar threatened historic sites around the country and telling the Chimayo story as part of a larger fight over development in culturally sensitive areas.

Our broader theme was also picked up by the *Los Angeles Times*, which sent a national correspondent to cover the story. The *LA Times* had written the "Chimayo, a little church where miracles happen" story several years ago. Now, they wrote it again, with a new angle: "Although not all land here is considered miraculous, it has always been precious," the story read. "Never more so than now, and small northern New Mexico towns—some of them over three hundred years old—are being overtaken by development that's marching inexorably from Albuquerque in the south to Taos in the north. Scores of local citizen groups are working to preserve the integrity of the region and their timeless, traditional way of life—especially at Chimayo. The church's cultural and historical significance has lent urgency to preserving the open space around it."

o   o   o

The success of the Chimayo mission story can be replicated with other land protection efforts, particularly if several factors are kept in mind:

1. *Reporters respond to stories, not facts.* In preparing material for the media, keep in mind that reporters, like all of us, respond

to human stories. The collection and recitation of facts—for instance, the particulars of a deal such as cost and acreage —are important, but only as "background" facts in a story. What reporters respond to is what we all respond to—stories about people and tales that tell the "why" of a place in addition to the details.

In thinking about how to tell a story that will interest the media, remember that the best selling points are details about the people who live on the land and their stories in their own words. We all remember stories we have read or heard, stories that moved us. It is those stories that the media are continually seeking; when we deliver stories that have emotional power, we can have them broadcast to a larger audience.

2. *Stories should be well timed.* One of the reasons the Chimayo story was successful was because it was tied to Easter. Traditionally, that is both a slow time for news events as well as a time when the media are looking for Easter-related stories, particularly "good news" tales. Had we pushed that story in mid-summer or later in the year, it is unlikely it would have been covered.

In thinking about the media potential for land acquisition stories, people working on these projects need to look at their efforts not only from the viewpoint of key decisions made in the acquisition effort, but also through the "big picture" lens of general news. For example, in the fall of the year, when students are returning to schools, the media are more likely to be interested in stories about preserving playgrounds and lands near schools that are used by students. Likewise, in the weeks before Memorial Day—the traditional kick-off of summer and vacation season —reporters are more interested in hearing about preservation efforts involving lands where families visit during the summer.

Another story "hook" involves history. Is a site historic? Does it have some connection to history or to an upcoming holiday? And in thinking about history, it doesn't have to be the type of history that is written about in books—it can be a simple community or cultural history illuminated through a well-told tale.

3. *Stories should be well thought out.* Most reporters are very busy. The more thorough and coherent are the printed materials in the press kit, the more likely it is that reporters will be interested. Printed material should be concise but also complete, including phone numbers of people who should be interviewed, reasons for interviewing those people, and some background on the individuals.

In thinking about how to pitch a story, one of the most useful practices is going through possible negative angles and putting together positive responses. Reporters are always interested in good stories, but by nature and training, they are often skeptical. They will often ask difficult questions, so if we have thought about those same questions beforehand and have come up with good answers, reporters are more likely to be interested in the story.

In addition, people working in our field need to think about how to answer the key questions all reporters will ask: "Why this story? Why now? Why should I cover this story instead of all the other stories that I could do?" Ultimately, the way that question is answered determines whether a story is picked up or ignored.

o   o   o

As another example of how important it is to think through stories, their history and broader context, as well as when to pitch them, following is the media coverage of a TPL project on Cat Island, Mississippi. This feature story was picked up by the *Washington Post* in November 2001.

Just two months after the terrorist attacks in New York and Washington, and in the midst of the Anthrax scare, the press was looking for "good news" stories to counteract grim front-page news. We pitched this story as an upbeat human interest story, and it ran on the front page of the Sunday paper. It makes use of many of the interviews we gathered for our press kit. We also carefully pitched this as a national story, raising awareness about TPL's preservation efforts around the country.

With Casinos Calling, Island Won't Cash In

By Sue Anne Pressley, *Washington Post* Staff Writer
(Sunday, November 11, 2001)

CAT ISLAND, Miss. —When U.S. Rep. Gene Taylor (D-Miss.) was a boy here on camping trips, he would look up at the bright stars and listen to the sounds of the wild creatures in the live oaks, and hope that nothing on this virtually untouched island in the Gulf of Mexico would ever change.

"Oh, Lord, as a little kid, you really expected to see a pirate walking around," he said. "It was always a thrill."

For generations, Cat Island — 2,000 acres, full-time population 1 —has been appreciated for its white-sand beaches, deer thickets and gator ponds, and other-worldly quality. As the largest remaining privately owned island left in the Gulf of Mexico, it also had begun to attract a different sort of attention in the last few years. Developers, including Gulf Coast gambling casinos, saw the T-shaped island about seven miles off the coast of Gulfport as a moneymaker waiting to happen.

But Cat Island is not destined to become Condo Island. The family that has owned the retreat since 1911 recently agreed to sell most of it to the nonprofit Trust for Public Land for $25 million. By January, the island will become the westernmost point of the Gulf Islands National Seashore, operated by the National Park Service.

As it turned out, Taylor was able to play a role in negotiations to save his boyhood haunt, as did Mississippi's Republican senators, Trent Lott and Thad Cochran, who helped get the first federal appropriations to finance the purchase. All have a sentimental interest in the place.

Cala Boddie Colbert, the great-granddaughter of Nathan Boddie, who bought Cat Island 90 years ago for $10,000, understands the attachment. Although her late father, also named Nathan, had lobbied to exclude the property from the national park when it was created in 1971, and envisioned more extensive development, Colbert and her two siblings took another approach.

"We have had a lot of different people express interest at different times. But we really believe the island should be preserved in its natural state," said Colbert, a New Orleans lawyer whose earliest childhood memories of Cat Island are of the "scary" free-roaming cattle that were later swept away by Hurricane Camille in 1969.

Colbert thought then, and still thinks now, that the island was magical, with its pirate legends, the still forests of slash pines and live oaks hung with Spanish moss, the sea birds flitting in and out, and the antique bits of pottery washed up on the shore, conjuring fantasies about the long-ago people who might have eaten from the dishes.

The island's dirt roads and trails are easily negotiable on caretaker Walter Gaudin's two-seat Kawasaki Mule. On a recent golden day, he showed off its many assets, including the pale sand dotted with horseshoe crabs and driftwood that stretches north–south for three glistening miles.

There is not a single cat on Cat Island—only a dog, a black Labrador named Hurricane—but French explorers who recorded the spot in February 1699 were struck by the abundant population of raccoons that ransacked the men's food stores every night. Thinking the creatures a type of cat, they named the island Chats-aux-huitres— cats with oysters—which evolved into today's name.

Over time, Cat Island saw its share of blood and derring-do. In the 1750s, French marines stationed there to protect New Orleans from British attack mutinied against their corrupt commander and shot him dead on the beach after he returned from a fishing trip. In the early 1800s, the island was the special playground of pirate Jean Lafitte, who used it as a way station for his ships carrying contraband and slaves to and from New Orleans.

During Prohibition in the 1920s, smugglers hid caches of whiskey in the island coves. After Colbert's great-grandfather bought it in 1911, the family looked the other way as friendly trespassers, including weekday shrimpers and weekend campers, ventured to the island and became enchanted.

But it was during World War II that Cat Island served perhaps its oddest purpose, reportedly becoming a secret government training ground for an experiment in whether dogs could be taught to sniff out the Japanese enemy. Japanese American soldiers from Hawaii, unapprised of their mission, were shipped in to don padded suits and dodge the dogs.

In a 1960s interview, Colbert's father said that he viewed the property as a "business investment," and dreamed of building a clubhouse, marina, airstrip and condominiums. Except for a canal and three large weather-beaten houses called fishing camps, though, nothing ever materialized.

With Boddie's death in 1985, and the beginning of riverboat casino development along the coast, the island's future became a more urgent question.

Boddie's son, George, an engineer, said he realized one morning about seven years ago that the family had a difficult decision to make when he and some friends went goose-hunting on the island's Goose Point. He turned, he said, to see two sailboats full of tourists, gaping in horror: "I thought, I ruined the morning for those folks. It was a wake-up call that times were changing, there are more people on the coast and they were going to be coming out here." Boddie never hunted on Goose Point again.

By 1998, Jerry Eubanks, superintendent of the Gulf Islands National Seashore, had heard that mainland casinos were interested in Cat Island and approached the family about inclusion in the park, which begins in the east at Fort Walton Beach, Fla. Soon, the Trust for Public Land became involved in the negotiations.

A nonprofit agency established in 1972, the Trust often steps in and buys property, holding it until the federal government or another entity has the time to approve the funding. The Cat Island project was particularly satisfying, Senior Vice President Alan Front said.

"I have been to Gulfport, and I have seen the flash of neon [of the casinos], and had Congress not appropriated this money and had the Park Service not been so forward-looking, the only person who would be going out to Cat Island would be the one spending time at a casino," Front said. "The casinos have the money—they don't have to wait until the next appropriations cycle."

There is a nice irony, however, involved in the long delay in the island's inclusion in the national park. If it had been part of the original plan 30 years ago, it would have been developed as "the centerpiece," Eubanks said, with the construction of extensive campgrounds and facilities; now, it is likely to stay "pretty much the way it is," he said. The Boddie family has retained 150 acres, and the fishing camps will remain.

As Cat Island's lone human inhabitant, it suits Walter Gaudin just fine if nothing here changes very much. He loves to play a flashlight across the canal at night and see only "the red eyes" of the alligators and other creatures.

A former tile layer who speaks in the musical cadences of his native New Orleans, Gaudin, 50, has lived here for five months, and has quickly learned to appreciate the solitude. He acknowledges that he is hardly roughing it, occupying one of the fishing camps outfitted with electric generators, cellular telephones and satellite TV. Visitors happen by every few days, and he makes it to the mainland once or twice a month in a 19-foot fishing boat.

And yet, the outside world can easily slip away: A bald eagle swirled overhead on a recent afternoon, and spotted deer crashed through the saw palmettos. Five alligators lined up in an interior pond, only their heads cracking the surface as they waited for some unsuspecting food to trip by. On the beach in the far distance, Gulfport was visible, but easy to ignore.

"I've had my share of fun in my life," said Gaudin, contemplating an evening meal of grilled redfish or speckled trout he had caught himself, with the dog and the nocturnal island animals as his company. "But if heaven is any better than this, I can't wait to get there."

Photographing Stories

| COURTNEY BENT

The way we photograph our relationships with the land must walk hand-in-hand with our purpose for sharing those stories. As documentary photographer Courtney Bent shows here with two TPL projects—Treetops in Connecticut and Griggs Farm in Massachusetts—images can do more than show a pretty landscape. They can also convey the human emotions felt for that place: the love, the familiarity, the fear of loss, and even the struggle.

Our visual stories should strive to show real people living real

lives, in the true documentary tradition of photography. Our new photography of land and people should suggest how people carry the land in their hearts and minds, and can help the observer see our relationship to land differently. It does this by including the wholeness of the human condition, conveying connection, conflict, sorrow, joy, love, and memory.

Because of her love of a mature forest in Greenwich, Connecticut, Louise Griswold left her private life behind and motivated over thirty organizations to campaign to save Tree-tops from development. This led to a Herculean ten-month long effort by the Trust for Public Land to raise $11.5 million to protect the 94-acre forest. Over 1,400 people donated to help protect this very special place.

Louise Griswold: "I was a part of something monumental, which I can't really understand but it gives me a great deal of hope for the future and hope for our community. I walk among the trees and say, 'O.K. I did it.' I remember at one point my husband saying to me, 'You act as if the forest has been waiting for you.'

"You can tell from the gray hair that I'm an old lady. So much has happened in the last few decades to shatter my idealism, and I did not want to end up being a cynical and bitter old lady. I saw

that appearances are deceiving, that things can be counter-manded with enthusiasm and perseverance. It's exhilarating. Saving Treetops probably has been the experience of my life. People have been remarking how it's been so wonderful to see all aspects of this town working together. And it was interesting. We couldn't have saved it without the very wealthy who have their own estates and we couldn't have saved it without the rank and file. And person after person has said that saving this forest united the town.

"Treetops is my sanctuary. This is where I come. This is my sanity. I'm thinking now that if this isn't a sacred place, it's coming pretty close. When you find a place like that, don't let it go."

When one of the last working farms in suburban Billerica, Massachusetts was slated to become another giant Wal-mart, the townspeople enlisted TPL's help to fight and save it. The Griggs family had been on that land for generations, and their farm was the place in town where people could still buy local produce and feel some connection to the valley's agricultural history.

Gil Griggs: "My ancestors grew up in Brookline, Massachusetts, all in Coolidge Corner. West Roxbury was given to my ancestors

PHOTOS: COURTNEY BENT

as a land grant in 1637. The odd thing was that in 1989 I helped start the farmer's markets in Massachusetts and we started the market right in Coolidge Corner, right where my father had farmed in 1890.

"The community here really came together because they realized the importance of saving the land. They saw what was happening in two or three other places where Wal-mart had bought land out from under a farmer and then proceeded to put all the local businesses underground as well. Folks just said 'enough is enough.' People in this town saw what was up, and they were willing to help keep my farm going. Since then the town has protected two other pieces of property, and who would have thought we could do that? Standing up for the land and for ourselves changed everything since."

A Few Earthy Words

| SCOTT RUSSELL SANDERS

In a speech delivered in 1952, Rachel Carson warned, "Mankind has gone very far into an artificial world of his own creation. He has sought to insulate himself, in his cities of steel and concrete, from the realities of earth and water and the growing seed. Intoxicated with a sense of his own power, he seems to be going farther and farther into more experiments for the destruction of himself and his world."

Carson voiced these worries before the triumph of television or shopping malls, before the advent of air-conditioning, personal computers, video games, the Internet, cell phones, cloning, genetic engineering, and a slew of other inventions that have made the artificial world ever more seductive. Unlike Earth, the artificial world is made for us. It feeds our bellies and minds with tasty pabulum; it shelters us from discomfort and sickness; it proclaims our ingenuity; it flatters our pride. Snug inside bubbles fashioned from concrete and steel, from silicon and plastic and words, we can pretend we are running the planet.

By contrast, the natural world was not made for our comfort or convenience. It preceded us by some billions of years, and it will outlast us; it mocks our pride, because it surpasses our understanding and control; it can be dangerous and demanding;

it will eventually kill us and reclaim our bodies. We should not be surprised that increasing numbers of people choose to live entirely indoors, leaving buildings only to ride in airplanes or cars, viewing the great outside, if they view it at all, through sealed windows, but more often gazing into screens, listening to human chatter, cut off from "the realities of earth and water and the growing seed."

The more time we spend inside human constructions, the more likely we are to forget that these bubbles float in the great ocean of nature. A decade before Carson issued her warning, Aldo Leopold, in *A Sand County Almanac*, recognized this danger as the central challenge facing the conservation movement: How do we nurture a land ethic in people who have less and less contact with land? How do we inspire people to take care of their home places if they feel no sense of place?

If we aim to foster a culture of conservation, we'll have to work at changing a host of things, from ads to zoos, from how we put food on our plates to how we imagine our role in the universe. Out of all these necessary changes, I wish to speak about one that is close to my heart as a storyteller, which is the need to root language once more in the earth. We need to recover the fertile meanings of words that arise out of our long evolutionary contact with dirt and wind, rivers and woods, animals and plants.

At the root of language, we often find an earthy wisdom. Take the word *growth*, for example. When Donella Meadows and her colleagues published a report in 1972 on the prospects for the continued expansion of the human economy, they called their book *The Limits to Growth*. The very title provoked outrage in many circles, because a prime article in the technoindustrial creed is that there are *no* limits to growth. According to this creed, any constraints imposed by nature will be overcome by technical ingenuity or the free market. Mining, drilling, pumping, clearing, plowing, manufacturing, and consuming—along with the human population that drives it all—will expand forever, the boosters claim. Politicians and business leaders speak of growth as unbounded and unambiguously good.

Our ancestors knew better. If we dig down to the root of growth, we find a verb that means to turn green, as grass does in the spring. In fact, *grow, grass,* and *green* all rise from the same Indo-European stem. Grass turns green in the spring, shoots up vigorously during the summer, then dies back and lies fallow through the winter. Season after season, the wilted grass turns to humus, enriching the soil. Molded into this word, therefore, is a recognition that growth is bounded, that it obeys the cycles of sun and rain, that it restores to the earth more fertility than it takes out.

If the phrase "sustainable growth" means perpetual expansion, then it is a delusion. Cancer shows that rampant growth soon becomes malignant. The sprawl of cities over the countryside and the spread of bellies over belts teach us that, beyond a certain point, expansion leads to misery, if not disaster. Nothing in nature expands forever. Certainly nothing on Earth grows unchecked, neither bodies nor cities nor economies. Buried in the word *growth* is the wisdom of people blessed with outdoor understanding, people who watched the grass rise and fall each year like a green wave.

o   o   o

The word *resource* embodies a similar insight. As we commonly use the word, it means "raw material," something we burn for energy, pulp for paper, or mine for steel. We speak of natural resources, human resources, financial resources, in each case referring to one kind of stuff that can be used to make other kinds of stuff. But the root meaning of *resource* is "to spring up again." *Source* and *surge* both derive from a verb meaning "to rise." A *re-source* is something that rises anew, like grass in a meadow or water in a spring.

In the world of hunters, gatherers, herders, and planters, what bounty surges forth time and again, year in and year out?

The light and warmth of sun, the life-giving water of rain and snow, the ebb and flow of tides; alewives and salmon returning to spawn; migrating bison and caribou; trees for canoes and shelters and fires; berries and seeds; fruits and nuts; corn and beans and squash; lambs, calves, children, and chicks. In traditional cultures, all these blessings were surrounded by ceremonies of respect, for people who lived on the bounty of nature understood the need to protect the source.

In light of this wisdom, fish in the sea are only a resource so long as their breeding grounds are preserved and their numbers are not decimated. Clean air and water renew themselves only so long as we do not fill them with poisons. Topsoil is a resource only so long as we do not sterilize it with chemicals or squander it to erosion. Coal, oil, iron ore, and the other materials we mine from the earth are not resources at all, because they can only be used up. Nor is money a resource, because it brings nothing into the world; it merely arbitrates the divvying up of what's already here. The wild abundance of the planet is quickly being exhausted because we have seized on nature's gifts without protecting the springs from which they flow.

o   o   o

Our obsession with money is evident in the way we normally speak of wealth, as if it could be measured by numbers in bank accounts and investment portfolios. But this is an anemic use of a word that carries a more robust meaning. *Weal* means "well-being," so *wealth* is a state of well-being. Trace *weal* and *well* and *will* back to their origins, and you find a single Indo-European verb that means "to wish or to choose." To be well, or to be wealthy, is to be in the condition we most desire.

Leaf through the pages of *Wealth* magazine or consult the "wealth-building" services of a financial broker, and you will learn how to increase your pile of dollars but not how to become happy or healthy or wise. Granted, in a cash economy one needs a certain amount of money in order to get by. Beyond that modest level, however, what else besides money do we need to achieve a state of well-being? I suspect that for many of us the list of things we most desire would include a thriving family, loyal friends, trustworthy neighbors, good work, wholesome food, a secure and comfortable home. Beyond our own private sphere, we might wish for safe streets, honest government, clean water and air, good schools and libraries, abundant parks and open lands, lively arts, a vigorous local economy, and a world at peace.

The grand old name for these shared sources of well-being is *commonwealth*. True wealth can never be wholly private any more than it can be wholly financial. No amount of money will insulate us from a degraded society or a devastated landscape. Dollars come and go. Stock prices rise and fall. The only forms of wealth that endure are those we possess and care for in common—the legacy of knowledge and skills, the humane institutions, the settlements and farms, and the fruitful Earth.

o   o   o

Just as we have taken too narrow and private a view of wealth, so we have taken too shallow a view of community. We speak of golf communities, resort communities, and online communities, as if they were places we could visit or leave at our whim. We speak of the scientific community, the religious community, and the international community, as if they were vast, vague, free-floating clubs we could join according to our professions or beliefs.

If we trace the word *community* back through *common* to its roots, we find that it derives from an Indo-European base meaning "to exchange or barter." The prefix *com-* means "closely alongside of or next to," suggesting intimacy. So *community* implies a mutual dependence and trust, as among neighbors who swap tools and seeds and stories, who return one another's wandering livestock, who look out for one another's children, who join together in raising a barn or harvesting a crop. In the original sense of the word, a community would be small enough for the members to encounter one another face-to-face; it would be grounded in a particular place; and it would derive its vitality from the circulation of goods, gifts, labor, and ideas.

The Amish have never forgotten the value of a shared life in a shared place. Before they take any action on their farms or in their households, they ask what effect it might have on the community. If it would hurt their neighbors or damage the soil or poison the wells, then it would be wrong, no matter if the action was convenient or profitable. Similarly, the Iroquois, when they meet in council, ask what might be the effects of their decisions on the descendants who will dwell in their homeland seven generations into the future. By posing these questions, the Amish and the Iroquois acknowledge that membership in community entails responsibility for preserving the health of a place.

o   o   o

To speak about the health of a place, as opposed to a person, goes against our customary use of that word. We talk about health clubs, health tips, health aids, and health professions, all with reference to preserving or restoring the fitness of an individual's body or mind.

But the word carries a larger meaning. *Health* comes from the same root as *hale, whole,* and *holy.* It means "complete, uninjured, sound." While a man or woman, a horse or tree in prime condition might be described as healthy, so might a free-flowing river, an old-growth forest, a loving family, a flourishing city, or a country at peace. We know, in fact, that a child growing up in a hateful family will suffer injury, as will a horse drinking from a polluted stream, or a tree drenched by acid rain. So the soundness of the part depends on the soundness of the whole. The health of individuals depends on the health of their households, communities, and homelands.

Like a healthy person, healthy land is vibrant, self-renewing, and lovely. It radiates a sense of integrity, all its parts gathering to form a resilient whole. We encounter such dynamic integrity not only in big wilderness but also in farms and forests that have been cared for through generations, in roadside ditches that simmer with butterflies, in streams that run with salmon, in schoolyard gardens and city parks. The radiance and vigor we behold in such places draws on the shaping energies of the entire Earth, and ultimately, through sun and moon and stars, on the cosmos. People who live in daily contact with wildness perceive this nurturing energy as holy. So they give thanks for food, for trees, for sunshine and rain, for breath. They honor the springs of life. They realize that only by protecting Earth's body can we protect the health and holiness of our own.

o   o   o

The most provocative word we have for the love that a person may feel for a place is *patriotism*. As we use the word nowadays —especially in the wake of the terrorist attacks on September 11, 2001—it arouses images of flags, soldiers, cemeteries, war memorials, and MADE IN AMERICA labels. Politicians pose for the cameras against a backdrop of stars and stripes, while declaring that patriotism means adherence to their own favorite policies. Advertisers tell us that patriotism means cruising the roads in our oversized cars, riding airplanes to vacation spots, investing in the stock market, running up debt on our charge cards, all for the sake of the American economy. Pundits and preachers identify patriotism with voting or with pledging allegiance or with regular attendance at church.

What is lost in all these uses of the word is the original meaning of *pater*-ism, which is love of one's fatherland. We might just as well speak of *mater*-ism, love of one's motherland. In either case, what's essential is the gratitude and devotion that a child feels toward the source of its life. And the source, here, is understood to be the land—not the leaders of the tribe, not the warriors, not the buildings or traditions of the clan—but the abounding Earth, with its creatures and cycles and seasons.

Imagine what our ancestors would think to hear us call ourselves patriotic for dropping bombs on foreign countries while each year thousands of tons of topsoil wash from our fields down the Mississippi River. Imagine what they would think of our bragging about the American economy as a beacon to the world while our forests and lakes die from acid rain, our rivers run foul, and our cities choke from smog. Imagine what they would think of those who invoke national security to justify drilling for oil in the Arctic National Wildlife Refuge while refusing to support more efficient use of the oil we already have. Where, in all of that, is the respect for Mother and Father America? How can we be patriots without loving and defending the land itself?

o   o   o

Like talk about patriotism, talk about security evokes military images—again, all the more so in the wake of the September 11 attacks. The sources of public security we hear about most often are the army, navy, air force, and police. The sources of private security we hear about are guns, alarms, and bank accounts. In the name of security, politicians offer us trillion-dollar missile shields, the Pentagon and their legions of contractors sell us newfangled weapons, developers peddle homes protected by fences and guards, car companies push four-wheel drive, and investment companies exhort us to grab a piece of the rock.

But are money and military force the best guarantees of our security? The words we've already examined suggest that our ancestors thought otherwise. In their original meanings, *growth, resource, wealth, community, health,* and *patriotism* all reveal an understanding that the well-being of people depends on the well-being of the land they share. Deplete the land, and you endanger the people. Those words also reveal an understanding that security can never be merely private, no matter how high the fences, no matter how large the net worth. Damage the commonwealth, and even the richest and mightiest individuals will suffer.

The word *secure* is made up of *se-*, meaning "free from," and *cura*, meaning "care or concern." Think of all that would be required to free us from care. True, we sometimes need warriors to defend us against attacks. But we also need to know that our children can play outside without danger, that we can safely drink the water and breathe the air, that we can count on a supply of nutritious food. We need shelter that's dry and warm. We need reliable neighbors. We need to trust that our jobs won't disappear at the whim of global corporations. We need to know that we'll be cared for when we fall sick and when we grow old. By these measures, tens of millions of Americans are insecure, and no additions to the Pentagon budget will free them from care. True security begins not with weapons but with membership in a loving community in a vibrant landscape, a community able to meet its basic needs from local sources, respectful of the weak as well as the strong, devoted to the well-being of all its members.

o   o   o

The word *conserve* rises from an Indo-European root meaning to "watch over, protect, or guard." Although it's the source of both *conservationist* and *conservative*, those who wear one label tend to be suspicious of those who wear the other. Both camps agree that some things are worth defending, but they disagree, often vehemently, over what those things are.

In the United States today, many people who call themselves conservatives defend a literal reading of the Bible, the authority of men over women, the freedom of landowners from legal restraint, the unimpeded growth of human population, the rights of gun owners and corporations, the privileges of private wealth. By contrast, those who call themselves conservationists fight to protect wilderness, watersheds, forests, topsoil, and other species, along with the knowledge necessary for preserving the health of the land.

Where the two camps might agree is on the need to defend

certain human values and inventions that have served us well through generations, such as close-knit families, small farms, locally owned businesses, neighborhood schools, frugality, simplicity, respect for the sacred, sound old buildings, moral responsibility, wise stories, and rich language. If we could agree that these are treasures worth preserving, then we might learn to cooperate in defending them. The cooperation would be good for both parties. Conservationists would be reminded that such human gifts are as vital as any wild gifts to the flourishing of our commonwealth. Conservatives would be reminded that no merely human goods can survive without the flourishing of wildness.

o   o   o

Some conservationists have shied away from describing their work as *stewardship*, because of the word's religious connotations. In the Bible, stewards look after property on behalf of a master—and the ultimate master of all property is God. As the Psalmist says: "The earth is the Lord's and the fulness thereof, the world and those who dwell therein; for he has founded it upon the seas, and established it upon the rivers." In the biblical view, a steward is one who takes care of the Creation out of love and respect for the Creator.

But *steward* has a secular meaning, as well. The word is compounded of *sty* and *ward*, so a steward is literally one who guards the pen where pigs or other livestock are kept. For a farming community, these animals mean a supply of meat, milk, cheese, wool, manure, skin, and bone. To be a steward, then, is a solemn trust, for the keeper of the sty is one who protects the source of food and clothing and fertilizer, perhaps for a family, perhaps for a village, perhaps for an entire people.

Although the religious version of *steward* is ancient and honorable, the secular version is the one we're more likely to agree upon. Whether or not we believe in a Creator, we can still feel reverence toward the Earth, we can still feel obliged to protect the sources of nurture and renewal for our communities. Instead of guarding pigs or sheep, in our time we're called to protect the soil, the air, the rivers and lakes, the forests and prairies, and the whole magnificent array of wild creatures.

o   o   o

The last of the words I'd like to examine here is *economy*, one of the most potent in our lexicon. For the good of the economy, we're asked to put up with unemployment, tax cuts for the rich, swollen military budgets, the draining of wetlands, the clear-cutting of forests, the damming of rivers, and countless other abuses of people and land. But all such arguments rely on a disastrously narrow understanding of *economy*. The word grows from two roots, the first meaning "house or settlement" and the second meaning "to govern or arrange." So economy means "the management of a household."

When we speak of economy, how large a house do we imagine? What belongs inside, within our care, and what belongs outside? As commonly used, *economics* refers to the distribution of goods and services through buying and selling. If you study economics, you will learn formulas to predict and track the movement of dollars, but you will not learn the effects of those dollars on the world. Whatever cannot be assigned a monetary value—such as the atmosphere, the oceans, the welfare of our children, the love of our friends, or the survival of other species —is excluded from this narrow definition of economy. By this reckoning, what matters most to our health and happiness belongs outside the house.

Our ancestors would surely have been puzzled by how much we omit from our economy. They invented this word before there was money to measure by. For them, to practice economy meant making sure that nothing was wasted and that everything needed for survival was looked after. They could afford to think only about the needs of their individual houses and their isolated settlements. In our homes and cities, we still need to make sure that nothing is wasted and that everything necessary for a decent life is looked after. The arts of managing a thrifty household are as crucial now as they've ever been. But in our far more crowded world, no walls can separate our homes and settlements from the fate of our neighbors or the fate of the Earth. We must enlarge our practice of economy to bring the whole planet within our care.

o   o   o

Depending on how we use it, language may distance us from sun and seed and soil, as Rachel Carson warned, or it may ground us more firmly in the earth. To gauge the difference, consider these celebrated lines from *A Sand County Almanac:* "We abuse land because we regard it as a commodity belonging to us. When we see land as a community to which we belong, we may begin to use it with love and respect."

Aldo Leopold uses the word *belong* here in two radically different ways. The first is economic, legal, and abstract; it's about claiming ownership and power. When I say that a city lot, a field, or a mountainside belongs to me, I set myself apart from the land, asserting my right to treat it as raw material for my own designs. The second use of *belong* is moral and emotional; it's about claiming kinship. When I say that I belong to this town or watershed or region, I'm declaring membership, as in a family, and I'm acknowledging my obligation to behave in a way that honors and protects the whole of which I am a part.

The first use of *belong* is about grasping, and the second is about being embraced. Thus the same word can either deny or affirm bonds of affection and responsibility between person and place. The choice we make between these rival meanings will dramatically influence how we treat the land.

o   o   o

The land does not belong to us; we belong to the land. Conservation begins from this plain and simple fact. But how do we persuade more people to feel the truth of it, to know it in their bones? Here's what the Kiowa writer N. Scott Momaday recommends:

> Once in his life a man ought to concentrate his mind upon the remembered earth, I believe. He ought to give himself up to a particular landscape in his experience, to look at it from as many angles as he can, to wonder about it, to dwell upon it. He ought to imagine that he touches it with his hands at every season and listens to the sounds that are made upon it. He ought to imagine the creatures that are there and all the faintest motions in the wind. He ought to collect the glare of noon and all the colors of the dawn and dusk.

A man or woman who ventures outside the human bubble and pays attention to a given landscape season after season, year after year, may eventually become a true inhabitant of that place, taking it in through every doorway of the body, bearing it steadily in heart and mind.

Only those who achieve such bone-deep familiarity with a place are likely to care for it as they would care for their children or parents or lovers. If we aim to nurture a practice of conservation, we need to cultivate this intimacy with land in ourselves, and we need to foster it in others. Every community, every watershed, needs people who feel responsible for that place, who know its human and natural history, who speak resolutely on its behalf.

As we speak up for the Earth, we should remember the exchange between Humpty Dumpty and Alice in *Through the Looking Glass*:

> "When I use a word," Humpty Dumpty said, in a rather scornful tone, "it means just what I choose it to mean—neither more nor less."
>
> "The question is," said Alice, "whether you can make words mean so many different things."

Clearly, we can't make words mean whatever we choose. Language is ornery and wild; it doesn't change at our beck and call. But we can work at restoring language, just as we can restore wetlands, rivers, and prairies. I've made my own small beginning at that work here. By examining a handful of key words from the struggle for conservation, I've tried to show how we might dig down through layers of cultural debris to uncover a buried wisdom. In order to bring the voice of the land into our councils and kitchens, we need to reclaim this evocative, sensuous, and earthy speech.

Halawa Valley | A Story of Coming Home

"Growing taro is an act of remembering." Glenn Davis says.[1] "Hawaiians are beginning to remember that we are organic and part of the land. It's essential for our culture to have places where we can go and remember who we are."

Glenn and Mahealani Davis[2] are sitting on a beach on the eastern end of Molokai Island facing the ocean at a wide, sweeping delta where it meets the river. A steep, narrow valley behind them leads to two large waterfalls. Halawa Valley was the first inhabited valley in Hawaii, and Glenn and Mahealani hold in their hands ancient adzes and fishhooks that they have found over the years. It wasn't until they found these ancient tools that they understood something about the people who had come before them. And then they realized that the valley was filled with overgrown terraces that were for growing taro, some of them several hundred years old. Glenn and Mahealani are typical modern Hawaiians. They didn't know much about their grandparents' traditions, and they felt largely disconnected from the land and their own culture. But the uncovering of the terraced fields, long abandoned, changed their lives forever. It was a big step toward knowing their culture again and finally returning home.

By connecting to our past through an experience of the land, we make sense of ourselves as part of a larger story.[3] Stories of our connection to the past enable us to feel at home in the present.

Glenn and Mahealani Davis have relearned Hawaiian traditions and are rebuilding Hawaiian culture by bringing young Hawaiians back to the taro fields. For thousands of years, until the 1950s, taro was a primary food on the islands. The culture developed in significant ways around the use of this plant. The Hawaiian word[4] for "family," *ohana,* is also the word for the taro root. *Kuleana* means both "land" and "responsibility." But many Hawaiians have left taro farming and the traditions of their ancestry for jobs in tourism.

With TPL's help, native Hawaiians are realizing a renaissance in their culture by going forward to the land and restoring a set of values that strengthens them as a people. TPL is working with two separate Hawaiian organizations, the Halawa Valley Taro Growers and the Cultural Learning Center at Ka'ala to help protect and make available again the *lo'i kalo* (taro paddies) as a method of sparking locally based community development. This conservation is helping Hawaiians to revive and teach the concept of the *ahupua'a*, a fundamental cultural practice that emphasizes how to care for the land.[5] Nurturing and understanding of the *ahupua'a* promotes the physical, mental, spiritual, social, and economic health and well-being of Hawaiian people.

Mahealani says, "Every *lo'i* opened up is an emotional experience for a Hawaiian. It's like a baby being born that belongs to everybody. People cry when it happens.[6] These taro fields show how really smart our ancestors were. The *lo'i* prove that you can build something that lasts. The world outside of this valley isn't like that. But you can't expect the world to change, you can only expect yourself to change."

For Glenn, returning to the taro fields is a process of returning to where he is most comfortable:

> Halawa is where you do the understanding. The history is all there imbedded in the land. We just needed to uncover it. But you can't protect that land alone; you can't do anything for that land without the human understanding. We know that this valley was waiting for the people and the understanding to return. Now that we've come

back, I mean, now that we've really come back and are committed to the taro again, there are more birds singing in the jungle. The water is flowing again. We have come home."

Notes

1. The goal is to convey the meaning of the project through someone else's words.
2. Allow the project to come alive by allowing it to be told by a person connected to that place. Help your reader/listener to understand and feel the place where the story lives.
3. Give the context for the project early on in the story sheet by answering the questions, Why is this project important? How does it fulfill our mission?
4. Articulating the connection between land and language is one of the most important and obvious ways we can explain the value of land to our culture. Language is essential to the practice of connecting land and people.
5. The story sheet should enable the reader to answer the questions, What impact will our mission have on the people served by our work? What larger social good are we achieving in our land conservation work?
6. The most powerful analogies come from people speaking easily and honestly about what they love. This analogy of comparing the *lo'i* to a baby being born came as a result of the interviewer (Peter Forbes) asking Mahealani to describe what that day felt like to her.

Sterling Forest | A Story of Economics

Saving land is often a story about good economics. The Trust for Public Land helped the people of New York and New Jersey protect more than 19,000 acres simply by explaining the cost of the alternative and negotiating a deal that cost less.

Sterling Forest lies on the New York–New Jersey border and is the home of diverse wildlife habitats with impressive biodiversity, as well as beautiful lake and mountain scenery. It serves as a link to other protected lands and surrounds seven miles of the Appalachian Trail. New York governor George Pataki, who led the effort to protect Sterling Forest, was quoted in the *New York Times* as saying: "To stand on top of Bear Mountain, to see Manhattan to the southwest and New Jersey to the southeast and now to have this unbroken string of wilderness preserved, is very gratifying. It will be important to future generations, and it is an opportunity that we will never have again."

When this land, only thirty-five miles from New York City, was in danger of becoming one of the largest development projects in the Northeast, what saved the forest was not solely the recreational or scenic value of the land, but also the economics. Thirteen thousand new homes as well as commercial and light industry and three golf courses

were going to be built there. The result would most certainly have been pollution of the watershed, which provides water to a quarter of New Jersey's population, or two million people. If the development plan had gone through, a new water filtration plant would have been needed, at a cost of $160 million. Not only did it make environmental sense to prevent the pollution of a drinking water resource, but it also eliminated the need for costly technological solutions.

The states of New York and New Jersey, the National Park Service, the Trust for Public Land, the Open Space Institute and other partners raised $55 million to buy and protect Sterling Forest. The protection of the property saves the public more than $100 million in filtration costs, and, in creating a new state park, it permanently preserves an enormous public resource that will benefit area residents and visitors to the park. An environmental education center and a visitor's center are being built to introduce others to and share information about this vital landscape. And all this is happening at about one-third of the public cost of the proposed development.

Few believed that there existed a wild area of the size and diversity of Sterling Forest within a one-hour drive of 26 million people. Nor could people imagine that protecting such a vast and enormously valuable natural resource could be considerably less expensive than the cost of developing it. Sterling Forest is a classic story of the multiple and diverse benefits that can be realized through a single conservation project.

Hiking by Flashlight

| JOHN ELDER

I've been poring over the annals of Bristol, searching for stories of how other families led their lives among these rocks, these woods. When Harvey Munsill died in 1876 he left a voluminous manuscript covering both the topography of his hometown and some of the main events in its first century. George III had chartered a township here in 1762, naming it Pocock after one of his admirals. But the French and Indian Wars made this a chancy locale for farming, and the only European settler before the Revolution was apparently a New York fugitive from justice who lived in a cave below the cliffs. The state legislature changed the name from Pocock to Bristol in 1789, and the Munsills and other founding families arrived over the following decade. As an old man in the 1860s, Harvey Munsill began to look back over the progress of the community, assembling lists of all who came to take the Freeman's Oath as citizens of Bristol, names and dates of the three churches' ministers, chronicles of the rise and fall of forges, kilns, and mills, and a registry of weddings, births, and funerals. In one section of the Munsill Papers, he also narrates early "Accidents and Incidents" that glinted as they settled through the slow, clear seasons of a still-unstoried town. This is the most eloquent chapter of his chronicle, and the one that I've searched most attentively in trying to read the character of my home.

The first "Incident" gives the somnolent pages of description a rough shake, making them tick like a clock, or like a heart.

Amze Higby a child between four and five years old son of Nehemiah Higby was killed by the fall of a tree cut by his father on the farm where Samuel Stewart and Eden Johnson first located and where William Dunshee now lives in the following manner, to wit,

The father Nehemiah Higby was chopping down trees for the purpose of clearing the land and the little sprightly boy was sent by his mother to call his father to dinner and when within a short distance of his father who was then chopping down a tree, with all the animation natural to a child of that age, called out to his father, dinner is on the table, and at that instant when first the father heard the voice of his little son, he discovered that the tree had commenced falling, and that to, in the direction of his beloved son who by the fall of that tree was instantly killed and this was the first death in Bristol.

This first death, like the expulsion of a long-held breath, was the beginning of the town's real history. The name Higby appears nowhere else in the tables of offices held, farms bought and sold. But when the child went down beneath the tree, a vital issue was decided. That settled things. For me, too, as with the old shepherd's loss of his son in the poem "Michael," this loss was an opening. I could enter sympathetically into the history of Bristol, grieving as a parent for the parents of Amze Higby, dead so young. The cycles of geology and of forest succession were humanized by personal cataclysm, brought into the scale of my human heart.

One other section in the "Accidents and Incidents" of Munsill's history rises to the intensity of Amze Higby's death, and again the central figure is a child.

Orcemus Shumway, about three years old, in the month of June 1806 wandered a way from home following the main travelled road, as is supposed, West from Bristol village to near the top of the hill, called Stoney Hill, and there taking a Woods road leading north into the Woods, and night coming on and dark the Child was unable to find its way home and remained in the Woods alone. Through the night although his anxious parents made diligent search to find him, but without success. Early the next morning notice was given that a Child was lost in the Woods.

This notice was sufficient to call out the inhabitants of Bristol old and young as well as some of the neighboring towns, and who immediately organized in to Companies and formed a line and commenced a march through the Woods, keeping at a proper distance from each other and making a thorough search which continued until about two o-clock in the after noon without making any discoveries; and the Search for a short time suspended, and all returned to the Village.

The Parents of the Child were almost frantic. The question was asked by many what can be done and the response from the many were Search until the Child is found. This seemed to be the unanimous expression, and they again formed in to Companies and formed a line, and by this time assistance had arrived from the neighboring towns and so increased their numbers as to enable them to form a verry extended line, which they did, and then commenced again to search the Woods where they had not before been, and after a diligent Search of about three hours the Child was found setting down by a large pine tree, some what frightened by the sight of so many strangers.

The Child was unhurt when found having followed the Woods road to the terminous and not able to find its way back being in a dense forrest and the Child to young to Exercise any judgement on the occasion. The Child was found a North Westerly direction from the Village.

When the fact was announced that the Child was found and unhurt, the declaration was reasserted with an earnestness that rent the air, and rolled back a rejoining echo, from the mountain, the Lost Child is found.

The writer was himself present on the occasion, and well remembers the good feeling manifested and smiling countenances of all who participated in the Search.

When I first came upon these two "Incidents" in Munsill, I immediately read them aloud as a pair to several friends. I wanted to share the satisfaction of the second Child's recovery, its effect enhanced by the earlier story's shocking loss. It reminded me of the story about when the mail-packet from England sailed into New York Harbor with the final installment of Dickens's *Old Curiosity Shop*. The crowd on the wharf, totally absorbed in the fate of Little Nell, called over the water to the Captain, "Is she dead?" When he shouted back "Dead," the crowd burst into tears. This time, though, the people of Bristol heard "The Lost Child is found," and couldn't stop grinning as they trudged back down to the village. This time the tree stood rooted in its place, sheltering the frightened Child until help came and carried him safely home.

o   o   o

Last week, on October 4th, our fourteen-year-old son Matthew did not come home for dinner at six o'clock. He'd told us that right after school was out he and his friend Benj Hanf were going up on the mountain to put some final touches on a "paleolithic shelter" they were building for their Global Studies class. They were doing a unit on human migrations and cultures in the first part of our present interglacial period, and the chance to fashion spears and other implements had engaged Matthew more than any other aspect of the new high school year. The two boys had built one shelter in a boulder-lea not far above Benj's house, but then forged farther up the broken slope. They'd found a steep overhanging cliff, above a ledge accessible only by a sketchy trail—the perfect hideout for two paleolithic teenagers. With wood and stones they walled in an enclosure against the cliff-face. With clay and chalk and charcoal they decorated the interior of their shelter with images inspired by the mystic hunters of Lascaux. Their original plan had been to bring the class up for a visit when it was completed, but as they switched to a more distant, more precarious site, they decided instead that they'd photograph the final project for a report. A camera and a box of chalk went up with them on this afternoon.

Seven o'clock came, and darkness, with no sign of Matthew. Benj's mother consulted on the telephone with Rita and me, uncertain what to do. Then, at 7:40, I drove to their house, taking a flashlight by which to hike up into the mountains after the boys. Benj's dad Bill was waiting for me by the road with his own flashlight, and together we started toward the rocky knob where he thought they might have gone.

The moon was long past full, and the night so overcast that except for the rippling pools of light around our flashlights total darkness prevailed amid the trees. I'd never hiked this approach to the ridge before, and could only follow Bill's lead. He paused often, looking for the remnant of a logging road that might lead us to the top. I had brought our retriever Maple, thinking she might scent the boys. She dashed around us, whirling up drifted maple leaves in the gusts of her excitement. The three of us ascended in a series of switchbacks until we reached a bouldery boil of land between two north-south ledges. Caves and cliffs were everywhere, still dripping from the afternoon's rain. Our flashlights swept into beautiful, fern-thick grottoes and, finding no lost boys, swung onward, leaving them to darkness.

Once we had made it to the broken height we started to call out for our sons as loudly as we could. "BENJ!" Bill would shout with his booming voice, a percussive call that bounced back to us from unseen cliffs. I sang out "Maaa-theww!" in my tenor, but the cadence always floated off unanswered through the lacy hemlock tops. Maple was such a panting, scrabbling noisemaker that it was hard at first to tell if there was any answer to our shouts. But as the minutes passed she began to stand absolutely still whenever either of us called, and to peer up into our faces as we held our breath, waiting with us for our sons' response.

Only at this point did I remember the stories of the two boys in Munsill's manuscript. In all my days of hiking and writing in the mountains, I had counted on recovering my bearings whenever I got lost. The wilderness all around our home had recovered from the ravaged, muddy slopes of the last century, and I held a familial faith in these providential woods. But what if, after all, Bill and I were hiking up into the *first* of Munsill's two stories, and my lost son were never found? More than once the two of us slid toward a cliff's edge with the collapse of an eroded slope. I began to picture a young body lying beneath a dark overhang, white face suddenly glowing in the flashlight's beam. I seemed to see myself from a great elevation, as well. My father had died seven weeks ago. Since then, my mother had fallen twice within her first day home from surgery. Now this? Dread fell with a rush like the sudden dropping of the temperature.

Bill and I had been climbing and calling, calling for hours, when we finally decided to head back down. Our consoling theory was that it was unlikely *both* boys would have been injured, and that if there had been some accident the uninjured boy would certainly have heard us by now and answered. Failing to receive any response, we therefore figured that either they'd made it safely down on their own or they'd wandered down the *eastern* flank of the mountain. If they weren't waiting at the bottom we'd call the police and fire departments and set up a search-and-rescue team. But in fact we heard a car on the road below, honking rhythmically to summon us home, when we were about halfway back to our starting point.

Benj's high-school-senior brother Brian and his friend Corey had found Matthew and Benj far to the north of where Bill and I were searching. When darkness fell, the two younger boys couldn't make their way out of their paleolithic world to the road and home. So they lit a fire, drew their light jackets around themselves, and settled into their shelter God-knew-where in the woods. Brian tracked them to their firelit lair, then mocked them safely home. Smoky, pale, and uncommunicative, two fourteen-year-olds waited for Bill and me in the headlights of the idling car.

After a microwaved helping of casserole, a glass of cider, and a shower, Matthew hit the sack, and so did Rita and I. I lay close to her side, trying to escape the chill as if sheltering by a fire-warmed overhang in the darkness of the mountain. But sleep did not come for a long time. I could still feel invisible rocks sliding beneath my boots as I walked down the slope defeated. My flashlight had given out on the return hike, so I'd had to follow closely behind Bill, trying to imitate him when he lifted one foot especially high or stepped to the side to avoid an obstacle. Struggling so hard to concentrate while going blind, I found that the trickling of unseen streams and the earthy smell of wet moss were magnified. And now, in the familiar darkness of our bedroom, I was filled with confused sensations, like a mountain brimming with recollection of the rain.

o   o   o

When an experience takes root in our lives it often grows up into a story. Just as I had wanted earlier to share the two tales from Munsill's history of Bristol, I now found myself telling people about the night of searching for Matthew and his friend by flashlight. The voice in my own ears when I told of this experience was a wry one—just another ridiculous incident in which we had managed to get involved. But a few days afterwards I was relating the search to a small group which included a man I'd never met before, and he heard something different in my voice. To judge by his response, he felt real fear within the humor of my story, and not just for the dangers of treacherous terrain after dark. More than I was conscious of myself, he focused on the struggle of parenting an adolescent whose inner life remained beyond the flickering beam of my flashlight and whose immediate future was still not so clear to me. This man's response was to put a poem by Wendell Berry into my mailbox the next morning. "The Way of Pain" begins,

> For parents, the only way
> is hard. We who give life
> give pain. There is no help.
> Yet we who give pain
> give love; by pain we learn
> the extremity of love.

The gift of this poem from a man I barely knew staggered me; it vaulted over the restraints of courtesy to touch the heart. The unknown, unseen listener was right. The point of my story, I realized now, was parenting and pain. I understood, too, that "a sense of place" would remain a vague concept if founded only in my researches into the natural and human history of Bristol. The galvanizing stories of place are finally those we suffer for ourselves.

In Leslie Silko's essay about stories and the Pueblo sense of place, she illustrates her points by telling two stories about the landscape around her home. One is an ancient mythic tale that ties the origin of a gigantic sandstone boulder to the Twin Hero Brothers' rescue of Yellow Woman from the giant Estrucuyo. But the other recounts an event that happened to Silko's own ancestors. "A high dark mesa rises dramatically from a grassy plain fifteen miles southeast of Laguna, in an area known as Swanee," this tale begins. Silko tells that her kinsmen were insufficiently wary while herding sheep near that mesa and thus allowed Apache raiders to surprise them from the other side, steal their sheep, and take their lives. To this day, her people never look at that landform without remembering the story of her careless relatives' murder, never tell the story without seeing that black mesa in their minds' eye.

Our Vermont landscape, like Silko's in New Mexico, begins to contain familial tales of loss. When a wilderness excursion was a self-contained idyll, a several-weeks' vacation from the pressures of job or school, the mountains remained serenely apart— a refreshing world elsewhere. But now that my hikes thread around and around the densely forested ridges of a plateau where our children are growing up, a new intensity and complexity has come into nature. I have an adolescent son I'm deeply worried about; I still feel as if I'm looking for him day and night in rocky terrain, with a failing flashlight; I hike the woods remembering other hikes, other days, and sometimes feeling cut off from my father and my son alike. But these gaps and fears also open a space for the local wilderness to rush into my daily life. Our family's years together here become more vivid because gathered into the mysterious circulation of the rocks and trees.

In the second and third stanzas of Berry's poem, the speaker reads in his Bible about sons and sacrifice—about Abraham and Isaac, and Christ crucified. In the fourth and final stanza he takes those stories into his dreaming heart.

> And then I slept, and dreamed
> the life of my only son
> was required of me, and I
> must bring him to the edge
> of pain, not knowing why.
> I woke, and yet that pain
> was true. It brought his life
> to the full in me. I bore him
> suffering, with love like the sun,
> too bright, unsparing, whole.

Abraham and Isaac, Michael and Luke. Tales of sacrifice cement our covenant with God and with the human community. But the covenant with land too calls for sacrifice, and may involve a loss. The story of young Amze Higby becomes a more concrete and immediate loss for me as I understand that my family, too, could lose our lives among these hills, will certainly lose them if we stay here through the seasons that call us home.

Caspar Headlands | A Story of Community

Climbing over the five-bar gate to follow a worn footpath over the Caspar Headlands toward the ocean, you walk through marsh grass and around clumps of dreaded gorse, past wild irises and the occasional brilliant red Mendocino paintbrush out to the edge of the bluffs. Small herds of deer roam the Headlands, and in certain seasons, sea lions bark mournfully and relentlessly on the rocks below. This is classic Mendocino coast: at any moment you can be enveloped in thick fog and swirling mist. Later the sun may break through and open up sweeping views across the ocean toward a distant horizon. Whales pass by on their journey from Alaska to calve in the warm waters of Baja California. Looking up above the beach to the bluffs of Caspar South, you see what might have become of the Caspar Headlands—sprawling houses with incredible ocean views, which block access to the coast for everyone else.

To call Caspar, California, a "town" would be a bit of an exaggeration for this rambling community of disparate and individualistic souls. As community leader Judy Tarbell says, "Caspar is a state of mind." Five years ago, when the major landowner in town decided to put much of the town and surrounding natural lands up for sale, Caspar residents barely knew one another. The threat of inappropriate development, particularly

in the Caspar Headlands, a beloved section of coastal and riparian land, was the catalyst that brought the town together. New connections between Caspar residents grew out of their discovery that they shared a love for the Caspar Headlands and out of their work to protect this land. Through five years of grappling with—and finding solutions to—concerns about the future development of the town, what was once a diverse and eccentric group of residents transformed into a tight-knit group of active citizens who call themselves the "Casparados."

Working together, the Casparados, TPL, the Mendocino Land Trust, and local and state organizations have protected the Caspar Headlands as a state park. Members of the town of Caspar are ecstatic because they have been successful in their efforts to preserve the Headlands for future generations, but they are also appreciative that they now have a real community that talks about and plans for the future. Mike Dell'Ara, the president of Caspar Community, the nonprofit organization formed to plan for the development of a sustainable Caspar village, has watched the changes to the community that came about through the process of conserving these lands. As he says:

> We've got a whole different community here today than we did three or four years ago. Certainly all the personalities are still there. But what has happened through this process is we've found and defined the things that we had in common rather than what made us different. And there were more things in common than we would have imagined.

Pond of Safety | A Story of Connection

"There are only 350 people in this community, and what links us together is our love of these mountains," says John Scarinza. "People come here because they're content to live in an isolated area and they pretty much want to be outside. Many of these folks came here as kids working in the huts and were taken by these mountains and never left. There's a series of trails that were created many years ago to link the guesthouses, church, and homes all together. The trails connect the community, and they get used every day of the year. They bring us outside and in touch with one another."

Walter Graff, David Willcox, and John Scarinza are very different people—an environmentalist, a community development expert, and a state trooper, respectively. They came together to protect Pond of Safety and the forest in the northern White Mountains of New Hampshire that has become their home. In many ways, they are the modern counterparts of three Continental army soldiers who escaped into this same wilderness and lived for two years at the edge of a spring-fed pond awaiting the end of the Revolutionary War. This forest was their refuge from their experience of the world. By 1796, these men had become upstanding citizens of Randolph, New Hampshire, the newly incorporated town that

had given them safety. Pond of Safety is the name that forever tells their story of refuge in a time of war.

David has traveled and lived all over the world working with many different cultures. Walter can identify everything in the forest. John, the state trooper, has a deep knowledge of the town and the law as well as an intuitive understanding and way of communicating with people. Working with their community, and with the Trust for Public Land, these three men helped to protect 13,500 acres that is both the forest and their home.

Most people collect postcards from the beautiful places they visit on their vacations. John Scarinza, the state trooper, collects postcards, old and new, of only one place: Randolph, New Hampshire, the town where he lives. John expresses his emotional connection to the land, his love for Randolph, with this postcard collection and through his words:

> What you accomplish up here in a rural area, people actually notice. It's hard to make a living here but being here is rewarding in its own way. Whether it is in law enforcement or anything else you do with your life, if you're in a city you can disappear and nobody knows you exist. That doesn't happen here. What I think we've done in this project is to try to preserve a way of life that exists where the people work with the land. People come to New Hampshire to see the White Mountains, not just to go to the Willow Street mall. But if this area gets developed like every other area, what's there to come visit? What will we have to keep us together, to call home?

Caretaking Tales

BEYOND CRISIS AND SALVATION

| WILLIAM CRONON

All too often it seems that the hard work of land conservation is done under crisis conditions. An important piece of real estate suddenly comes on the market, or is threatened with development, or is subject to new government policies, or in some other way demands our urgent attention. So we roll up our sleeves and get to work, raising money, building coalitions, purchasing easements, invoking legal precedents, organizing political support, cutting deals—all the necessary tasks without which few acres would ever receive the protection they deserve. The goal of saving land for the public good could hardly be more important, and there is nothing sentimental about it. Successful land conservation is rarely achieved without consummate technical expertise and hard-nosed realism.

It may thus seem a little counterintuitive, if not downright perverse, to assert that nothing is more vital to the success of land conservation than the stories we tell about it. In the midst of raising millions of dollars and making complex deals with power brokers, why on earth should we waste time on something so seemingly intangible and trivial as storytelling? Surely busy land conservationists have more important things to worry about.

But in fact nothing could be more essential. Stories are the indispensable tools that we human beings use for making sense of the world and our own lives. They articulate our deepest values and provide the fables on which we rely as we confront moral dilemmas and make choices about our every action. Here is a new situation: What should we do? The answer, repeated in infinite variations, always takes the form of a narrative. If we do *this*, then *that* will follow, and we judge our actions good or bad by the chains of cause and effect we thus set in motion. Just so do stories provide the interpretive compass with which we navigate our lives.

A moment's reflection will confirm that even the practical day-to-day work of land conservation is full of storytelling. Why should this donor give money for the purchase of this land? Because doing so will set in motion a story in which the donation makes possible the purchase, and the purchase in turn embodies values about which the donor cares enormously. Why should this politician throw her weight behind this project? Because doing so enables her to author a story that demonstrates for future audiences (and also for herself) the kinds of actions and commitments she can be counted on to support. Why should people in this community wish to preserve this green space as a park? Because the park will then provide the scene for countless future stories about the children and families and lovers and lone souls who will find affirmation in that place.

There is nothing trivial about such stories. Indeed, one might even say that natural ecosystems and abstract geographical spaces become human *places* precisely through the accumulation of narratives that record and pass on to other people the living memory of what those places *mean*. Stories *create* places by teaching us why any given patch of earth matters to the people who care for it.

If this is so, then what kinds of stories should land conservationists tell about the places they seek to save? What sorts of values and meanings do we want our stories of these places to affirm?

The very nature of this work means that all too often we find ourselves telling *crisis stories*. Here is a precious place, and here are the awful things that are about to happen unless we immediately do something to save it. A key attraction of crisis stories is the urgency they convey: the more compelling the crisis they narrate, the more desperate the call to action. An equally important appeal is that crisis stories call upon listeners to assist in authoring a completely different narrative in which the impending tragedy is transformed into its opposite by changing the anticipated ending. The purpose and power of crisis stories, after all, is their ability to metamorphose into *salvation stories*.

This is in fact one of the oldest narrative traditions in Western culture, going all the way back to the Hebrew prophets who foretold disaster if the Jews did not mend their ways in time to avoid the wrath of a just God, thereby altering the end of the prophet's story. Here is a crisis—in most instances, a crisis that our own bad conduct has precipitated. Here is what we must do to avert disaster. Here is what we will gain if our heroic efforts succeed. In just this way do crisis and salvation complement and complete one another. In American conservation history, places whose meanings have been defined by stories of crisis and salvation include such famous names as Hetch Hetchy, Echo Park, and Glen Canyon. But in fact every successful and unsuccessful land conservation battle reenacts these same narratives of paradise lost or paradise regained.

However compelling these prophetic narratives of crisis and salvation may seem, and however effective they often prove as tools for organizing, we should recognize that their very power also entails risks. For one, people can stand only so many crises before exhaustion or disbelief sets in. Under ordinary circumstances, daily life does not present itself as an unrelenting string of crises. If someone insists on telling us stories that suggest otherwise, in which every environmental problem or land conservation challenge threatens impending doom, we eventually doubt the storyteller and begin to think of the boy who cried wolf.

Even more important, the same promised salvation that makes crisis stories so attractive can also convey deeply misleading ideas about the nature of conservation. Yes, it sometimes does happen that dramatic action needs to be taken to "save" a given tract of land from threats that might otherwise do it serious harm. But triumphing over these urgent threats brings neither the transcendent salvation nor the narrative closure that our stories tempt us to expect. The real life of real places never "ends" the way stories do.

Instead, the end of the crisis is almost always the beginning of a very different story about the much subtler challenge of *caring* for the land, day in and day out, with no end in sight. We're not nearly so good at telling this kind of story. It's much more exciting to cast ourselves as heroes in a dramatic struggle to "save" a place we care about. But once it has been "saved," the heroic story we've just enacted can tempt us to move on in search of the next dramatic struggle, forgetting that the real work of caring for the place we've just protected will start again tomorrow, and the day after that, and the day after that, forever. Real life and real places are like this, even if stories are not.

Narratives of crisis and salvation entail at least one additional risk as well. Far more often than not, the places we seek to protect are cast in such stories as "natural," whereas the forces that threaten them with destruction are cast as "human." There are plenty of good reasons for this, given the cleverness and zeal with which human beings can sometimes muck up the world around them. But if the only stories we tell are ones in which natural victims are threatened by human villains, and the only honorable human response is to "protect" nature by isolating it from further human interference, then we may want to worry just a bit about the moral lessons such fables teach about humanity's place in nature.

Salvation stories in which a natural landscape is spared from human use or restored to organic health in the wake of human damage can imply that most of the things people spend the bulk of their time doing—building comfortable homes, raising happy children, doing honest work, consuming good food, enjoying life—represent "damage" from nature's point of view. If the ultimate implication of a crisis story is that humanity is an awful wound from which nature must somehow heal, can we claim to be offering any constructive vision of a better human way of living and working with nature? What sources of hope and self-respect do we expect a child to find in such fables?

For all these reasons, we need more than just narratives of crisis and salvation if the work of land conservation is to succeed in the long run. The most helpful stories may actually begin right after a crisis has been resolved and a tract of land has been "protected." The high drama may be over, but the ongoing work of sustaining the land for which we are now responsible has just begun. To help guide our lives beyond the crisis, we need to become better at *caretaking tales* that celebrate the quieter forms of heroism in which people commit themselves to nurturing a place and its inhabitants, human and nonhuman alike, for all time to come.

Such stories will focus on themes that tend to be less visible in narratives of crisis and salvation. They inevitably involve continuing *relationships* between people and the natural world, so that *connections* rather than *dis*connections play more central roles. Just as important, they show people *working* in and with natural systems to sustain those systems for the long run. Working for the good of a whole that contains rather than excludes a human presence means recognizing that natural systems are in fact *communities* to which we ourselves belong. Acknowledging our membership in—and dependence upon—such communities is the necessary precondition before we can take responsibility for them. *Narratives that celebrate connections and relationships in communities that we ourselves are responsible for* *nurturing and sustaining:* it was precisely these kinds of stories that Aldo Leopold was advocating when he penned his famous words, "We abuse land because we regard it as a commodity belonging to us. When we see land as a community to which we belong, we may begin to use it with love and respect."

Love and respect: surely these are the core moral values that the storytelling work of land conservation must celebrate and affirm. It's worth noticing that neither of these crucial words can ever describe individuals or people in isolation from the rest of the natural world. Both are inherently relational, and both describe the emotions from which our sense of obligation and responsibility and community toward the rest of nature ultimately flows. Utopian though it might seem, if we could become steadier in our practice of such values, not only might we become better at telling caretaking tales, but our need for stories of crisis and salvation might diminish as well.

This leads to one final observation about the stories we tell in the work of land conservation. Almost always, and for the best reasons in the world, our stories focus narrowly on lands we are trying to save: a wilderness on the north slope of Alaska, a grassland with oil beneath it near the front range of the Rockies, a family farm threatened with subdivision on the outskirts of Chicago, a community garden in Harlem. Certainly we must tell compelling stories about such places.

But caretaking tales—tales of love and respect, of belonging and responsibility—in fact need to be told about *all* the lands of this good earth, including those where people earn their livings and make their homes. Not just wildernesses and parks and public green spaces need our celebration. So too do cities and suburbs, farms and ranches, mines and industrial forests, factories and homes. It's not just that the wildernesses and parks and green spaces will be destroyed by forces emanating from these other places if we don't do a better job of witnessing and taking responsibility for the relationships that bind all of them together. It's also that we human beings need to find honor and self-respect for ourselves and our children as much in our homes and workplaces as in the lands we set aside as special. We need caretaking tales for all of them together, because only then can we hope to find true salvation for them all.

About the Contributors

TIM AHERN was press secretary for Interior Secretary Bruce Babbitt before joining the Trust for Public Land as the Director of Media Relations. He was also a long-time correspondent for the Associated Press.

COURTNEY BENT is an award-winning photographer based in Cambridge, Massachusetts. She is known for her documentary and portrait photography, and for her passion for capturing images "behind the scenes." Courtney teaches at the Charles River Creative Arts Program, one of the nation's leading arts programs for children.

WILLIAM CRONON is the Frederic Jackson Turner Professor of History, Geography and Environmental Studies at the University of Wisconsin-Madison. An award-winning writer of environmental history, his books include *Changes in the Land*, and *Nature's Metropolis.*

JOHN ELDER is a professor of both English and environmental studies at Middlebury College in Vermont. His books include *Reading the Mountains of Home* and *The Frog Run*. Elder is also an advisor to Stories in the Land, a program of environmental education through the Orion Society.

PETER FORBES is the director of TPL's Center for Land and People, a photographer, and the author of *The Great Remembering: Further Thoughts on Land, Soul, and Society*. He farms with his family in the Mad River Valley of Vermont.

BARRY LOPEZ is the author of many works of fiction and nonfiction, including *Crossing Open Ground*, *Of Wolves and Men*, *River Notes*, and *Arctic Dreams*, for which he was awarded the National Book Award. He lives in rural Oregon.

WILL ROGERS is president of the Trust for Public Land. Before becoming TPL's president, Will directed programs that led to the conservation of such diverse natural resources as Volcan Mountain in San Diego's backcountry, He'eia Kea Valley in Hawaii, and Skyline Ranch in the Oakland Hills. Will lives with his family and keeps bees in Berkeley, California.

SCOTT RUSSELL SANDERS is Distinguished Professor of English at Indiana University. He has published seventeen books, including novels, essay collections, and children's books. Among his books are *Staying Put, Writing from the Center* and *The Paradise of Bombs.*

HELEN WHYBROW is a freelance editor, writer, and publishing consultant. For six years she was the director of The Countryman Press, a division of W. W. Norton. Her most recent project, *Dead Reckoning,* an anthology of nineteenth-century adventure writing, will be published later this year.

For Further Reading

Berry, Wendell. 2000. *Life is a Miracle: An Essay Against Modern Superstition.* Washington, D.C.: Counterpoint Press.

——. 1998. *The Selected Poems of Wendell Berry.* Washington, D.C.: Counterpoint Press.

——. 1993. *Sex, Economy, Freedom and Community: Eight Essays.* New York: Pantheon.

——. 1995. *Another Turn of the Crank.* Washington, D.C.: Counterpoint Press.

——. 1989. *The Hidden Wound.* San Francisco: North Point Press.

——. 1981. *Recollected Essays 1965–1980.* San Francisco: North Point Press.

Bellah, Robert N., et al. 1985. *Habits of the Heart: Individualism and Commitment in American Life.* Berkeley: University of California Press.

Bookchin, Murray. 1982. *The Ecology of Freedom: The Emergence and Dissolution of Hierarchy.* Palo Alto, Calif.: Cheshire Books.

Crawford, Stanley. 1992. *A Garlic Testament: Seasons on a Small New Mexico Farm.* New York: E. Burlingame Books.

Cronon, William. 1983. *Changes in the Land: Indians, Colonists, and the Ecology of New England.* New York: Hill and Wang.

deBuys, William, and Alex Harris. 1990. *River of Traps: A Village Life.* Albuquerque: University of New Mexico Press.

Dillard, Annie. 1982. *Teaching a Stone to Talk: Expeditions and Encounters.* New York: Harper and Row.

Eisenberg, Evan. 1998. *The Ecology of Eden.* New York: Alfred A. Knopf.

Elder, John. 1998. *Reading the Mountains of Home.* Cambridge, Mass.: Harvard University Press.

Fischer, Louis. 1950. *The Life of Mahatma Gandhi.* New York: Harper and Row.

Freyfogle, Eric. 2001. *New Agrarianism.* Washington, D.C.: Island Press.

——. 2000. "A Sand County Almanac at 50." *ELR News and Analysis.* Washington, D.C.

——. 1998. *Bounded People, Boundless Lands.* Washington, D.C.: Shearwater Press/Island Press.

Jackson, Wes. 1994. *Becoming Native to this Place.* Lexington: University Press of Kentucky.

Hogan, Linda. 1995. *Dwellings: A Spiritual History of the Living World.* New York: W. W. Norton.

Kellert, Stephen R. 1997. *Kinship to Mastery: Biophilia in Human Evolution and Development.* Washington, D.C.: Island Press

Kemmis, Daniel. 1995. *The Good City and the Good Life.* New York: Houghton Mifflin.

Kunstler, James Howard. 1993. *The Geography of Nowhere: The Rise and Decline of America's Man-Made Landscape.* New York: Simon and Schuster.

Leopold, Aldo. 1999. *For the Health of the Land: Previously Unpublished Essays and Other Writings.* Edited by J. Baird Callicott and Eric T. Freyfogle. Washington, D.C.: Island Press.

———. 1986. *A Sand County Almanac.* New York: Ballentine Books (New York: Oxford University Press, 1966).

Logsdon, Gene. 1993. *The Contrary Farmer.* Post Mills, Vermont: Chelsea Green Publishing.

Lopez, Barry. 1988. *Crossing Open Ground.* New York: Scribner's.

Macy, Joanna. 2000. *Widening Circles: A Memoir.* Gabriola Island, B.C.: New Society Publishers.

———. 1991. *World as Lover, World as Self.* Berkeley, California: Parallax Press.

McKibben, Bill. "How Much is Enough? The Environmental Movement as a Pivot in Human History." Harvard Seminar on Environmental Values, October 2000.

Meadows, Donella H. 1991. *The Global Citizen.* Washington, D.C.: Island Press.

Momaday, N. Scott. 1997. *The Man Made of Words: Essays, Stories, Passages.* New York: St. Martin's Press.

Nabhan, Gary Paul. 1997. *Cultures of Habitat: On Nature, Culture, and Story.* Washington, D.C.: Counterpoint Press.

Nash, Roderick. 1989. *The Rights of Nature: A History of Environmental Ethics.* Madison: University of Wisconsin Press.

Nearing, Helen, and Scott Nearing. 1989. *Living the Good Life: How to Live Sanely and Simply in a Troubled World.* (Originally published 1954.) New York: Shocken Books.

Pollan, Michael. 2001. *The Botany of Desire: A Plant's Eye View of the World.* New York: Random House.

———. 1991. *Second Nature: A Gardener's Education.* New York: Atlantic Monthly Press.

Pyle, Robert Michael. 1993. *The Thunder Tree: Lessons from an Urban Wildland.* Boston: Houghton Mifflin.

Sanders, Scott R. 1993. *Staying Put: Making a Home in a Restless World.* Boston: Beacon Press.

Schumacher, E. F. 1979. *Good Work.* New York: Harper and Row.

Silko, Leslie Marmon. 1977. *Ceremony.* New York: Viking.

Snyder, Gary. 1990. *The Practice of the Wild: Essays.* San Francisco: North Point Press.

————. 1995. *A Place in Space: Ethics, Aesthetics, and Watersheds, New and Selected Prose.* Washington, D.C.: Counterpoint Press.

Stegner, Wallace. 1998. *Marking the Sparrow's Fall: Wallace Stegner's American West.* New York: Henry Holt.

Swimme, Brian. 1996. *The Hidden Heart of the Cosmos: Humanity and the New Story.* Maryknoll, New York: Orbis Books.

Thoreau, Henry David. 1958. *Walden.* New York: Harper Classics (Boston: Houghton Mifflin, 1854).

Turner, Jack. 1996. *The Abstract Wild.* Tucson: University of Arizona Press.

White, Richard. 1995. "Are You an Environmentalist, or Do You Work for a Living?" In *Uncommon Ground,* edited by William Cronon. New York: W. W. Norton: 239–243.

About the Center for Land and People

NEW IDEAS FOR CONNECTING LAND AND PEOPLE
THROUGH CONSERVATION

How can we make conservation more effective, not only for preserving land but also for nurturing community? While we have saved millions of acres, Americans seem less connected to the land than ever before. Our best hope is to work for a shift in American culture. By inviting citizens to imagine their lives differently, by offering them new ways of dwelling in the land, we can help replace the culture of exploitation with a culture of conservation.

The Center for Land and People works to create a greater understanding of the many benefits that flow from a respectful relationship with the land: human health, ecological health, economic sustainability, enriched community life, companionship and fairness between humans and other species, and the renewal of the human spirit. By linking changes in the land with changes in people, we seek to enlarge the impact of conservation, carrying it beyond the measure of acres and dollars—important as those are—to the measure of social and individual well-being.

We conserve land because of core values including respect, gratitude, generosity, compassion, the desire for belonging, and love. Land conservationists can expand these values into culture by revealing them more courageously and explicitly in each project. The Center seeks to advance a practice of land conservation that demonstrates more joyful, responsible, conserving ways of living.

The programs of the Center for Land and People include:

- *Redefining Success:* helping conservationists to redefine success for the movement by creating and piloting new ways of measuring the impact and benefits of conservation to a healthy society.

- *Mission Exploration:* creating forums for deeper conversations about the core values and purpose of land conservation, so that the movement as a whole can be more thoughtful and deliberate and in service to its highest aspirations.

- *The Story Project:* helping the conservation movement tell stories that illustrate the meaning of land in peoples' lives and in the life of a community.

- *Publishing:* working to advance new voices and strategies for the conservation movement through widely distributed books and other media.

- *Rethinking the Promise:* convening a series of learning dialogues between writers, artists, social critics, academics, and conservation activists to share ideas and innovations about how conservation can help people think and act differently.

Other books from
The Center for Land and People

Our Land, Ourselves
Readings on People and Place

A collection of diverse readings on the many themes of people and place—themes such as the protection of wilderness and the idea of the wild, the nature of home, the purpose of work, and the meaning of community. These voices suggest a new way of viewing land conservation as the process of building values and positively shaping human lives.

ISBN 0-9672806-0-5 | 240 pages | $16.95

The Great Remembering
Further Thoughts on Land, Soul, and Society

An activist's exploration of the meaning of land to our culture, this book is also a call to land conservationists to redefine the promise of their work as the building of relationships between land and people.

ISBN 0-9672806-1-3 | 112 pages | $14.95

Both of these titles can be ordered from
Chelsea Green Publishing Company.

Call 1-800-639-4099 or find them online at:
www.chelseagreen.com

For a complete list of publications from
the Trust for Public Land, go to **www.tpl.org**